Que® Quick Reference Series

Hard Disk
Quick Reference

P. D. Moulton
Timothy S. Stanley

Que Corporation
Carmel, Indiana

Library of Congress Catalog Number: 88-63856

ISBN 0-88022-443-6

92 91 90 89   4 3 2

Interpretation of the printing code: the rightmost double-digit number is the year of the book's printing; the rightmost single-digit number, the number of the book's printing. For example, a printing code of 89-4 shows that the fourth printing of the book occurred in 1989.

This book is based on DOS Versions 3.3, 4.0, and 4.01.

Que Quick Reference Series

The *Que Quick Reference Series* is a portable resource of essential microcomputer knowledge. Whether you are a new or experienced user, you can rely on the high-quality information contained in these convenient guides.

Drawing on the experience of many of Que's best-selling authors, the *Que Quick Reference Series* helps you easily access important program information.

Now it's easy to look up often-used commands and functions for 1-2-3, AutoCAD, dBASE IV, WordPerfect 5, Microsoft Word 5, and MS-DOS, as well as programming information for Assembly Language, C, Turbo Pascal, and QuickBASIC 4.

Use the *Que Quick Reference Series* as a compact alternative to confusing and complicated traditional documentation.

The *Que Quick Reference Series* also includes these titles:

1-2-3 Release 3 Quick Reference
1-2-3 Quick Reference
Assembly Language Quick Reference
AutoCAD Quick Reference
C Quick Reference
DOS and BIOS Functions Quick Reference
dBASE IV Quick Reference
MS-DOS Quick Reference
Microsoft Word 5 Quick Reference
QuickBASIC Quick Reference
Turbo Pascal Quick Reference
WordPerfect Quick Reference

Publishing Manager
Lloyd J. Short

Product Director
Karen A. Bluestein

Editor
Sandra Blackthorn

Technical Editor
Jeff Booher

Editorial Assistant
Fran Blauw

With Contributions by
Mark Minasi

Proofreader
Peter Tocco

Indexer
Sharon Hilgenberg

Table of Contents

Introduction

Designed as a general guide, the *Hard Disk Quick Reference* shows you how to avoid and correct serious errors in hard disk installation and setup, and provides key information for organizing your disk for optimum use. The *Hard Disk Quick Reference* outlines and describes the procedures for installing your hard disk. These procedures are a compilation of the procedures for the many varieties of hard disks on the market today for PCs, XTs, and ATs, and for the few types of hard disks for PS/2s. This book gives you the essential information necessary to avoid the many pitfalls encountered in hard disk installation and setup.

The setup tips show you how to avoid erasing or destroying your essential data. Suggestions for effective hard disk maintenance and backup techniques are presented to ensure a long, error-free life for your hard disk. Batch files are explained for streamlining your hard disk use. Error messages are detailed for your convenience. And three sample hierarchical structures are presented at the back of this book to assist you in organizing your hard disk.

This *Hard Disk Quick Reference* guide provides only general hard disk information, and as such, it is not intended to be a replacement for the detailed information provided by hard disk manufacturers or information found in Que's *Managing Your Hard Disk*, 2nd Edition. You should supplement the information in this book with one of Que's more complete DOS or hardware books, such as *MS-DOS Users Guide*, 3rd Edition; *Using PC DOS*, 3rd Edition; *DOS Tips, Tricks, and Traps*; *Managing Your Hard Disk*, 2nd Edition; or *Upgrading and Repairing PCs*.

Notations Used in This Guide

When DOS commands are specified in this guide, the command that must be typed is presented in **boldface blue** type and the information appearing on the PC's screen is shown in `this type`. For example, the CHKDSK command would appear as follows:

CHKDSK

The following screen is produced when you enter this
command:

```
C:\ >CHKDSK

32882688 bytes total disk space
57344 bytes in 3 hidden files
102400 bytes in 40 directories
29263872 bytes in 1147 user files
3459072 bytes available on disk

720896 bytes total memory
149232 bytes free

C:\ >
```

Words in UPPERCASE letters in **boldface blue** type are
mandatory and must be entered; any words in *italics* are
optional or variables used for modifying the command.
In entering these commands, be sure to substitute the
correct disk letter, path specification, file name, etc., for
the *italicized* variables shown.

HARD DISK BASICS

This section explains how hard disks function. It
provides the essential descriptions of the technical
terminology used for hard disk operations and how DOS
works with hard disks.

What Is a Hard Disk?

A hard disk system is usually two or more rigid metal
platters enclosed in a hermetically sealed case that stores
data by magnetic encoding similar to that of a floppy
disk or a cassette tape. Hard disks, floppy disks, and
cassette tapes all store data by rearranging the magnetic
properties of the storage medium to create
representations of data. They all have specially designed
read/write heads to write the data to the storage medium
and to read that data as desired by the user.

However, hard disks provide much greater storage capacity and data access performance than do floppy disks. Unlike floppy disks, the disk platters or media are generally not removable from the hard disk—hence the name fixed disk (see fig. 1).

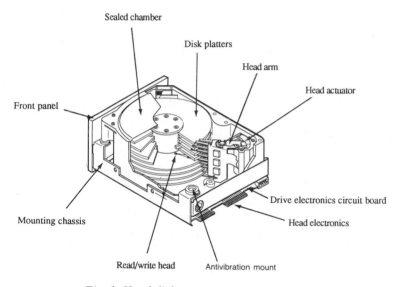

Fig. 1. Hard disk anatomy.

DOS Versions 2.0 and later have been designed to manage the increased storage capacity and numbers of files on a hard disk. This capability gives you much greater convenience because your working data is now readily available. With this increased convenience comes a price: greater care must be exercised in setting up, organizing your data on the hard disk, and maintaining backups.

All hard disks reduce the need for you to store data on floppy disks (although you still need to perform regular backups of your hard disk data) and provide you with the ability to transfer information rapidly between the Random-Access Memory (RAM) and the hard disk, where the data can be stored permanently. You can store many files on the hard disk, but this will result in the inherent risk of losing valuable data when mistakes are made or failures occur. Further, effective use of the disk requires a disciplined layout of the file structure on the disk and periodic file management and maintenance. Time spent organizing the disk and removing old files cannot be avoided.

A hard disk acts just like an orderly file cabinet next to your desk. It is a repository for the information with which you work. If you leave all your paper files on your desk, you have to look at each one to find the file you need. Soon your desk becomes cluttered. Placing the files in an orderly file cabinet will reduce this clutter. You may quickly locate and retrieve the information stored there.

Think of your hard disk as an electronic filing system, capable of storing large amounts of information in a very small space. Because information in electronic form can be stored quickly and conveniently, computer files are created at a much greater rate than paper files. Hard disks become inundated with files, necessitating constant data management and removal of seldom-used files. Many commercial and public domain software programs are available to help manage your hard disk. However, the focus here is on those software tools provided by DOS because they are most readily available. You can use the DOS tools to make your hard disk well organized, which enables you to work faster and more efficiently.

Hard Disk Data Storage

Data storage on a hard disk is similar to storage on a floppy disk. A double-sided double-density floppy disk has data placed in 40 concentric circles called tracks. When a floppy disk is formatted, 9 sectors (sections of the disk) are created in each track to hold the data stored there. Each sector can hold 512 bytes (characters) of information. Data is read from the tracks and sectors by a read/write head that moves across the disk to specific locations on that disk. One read/write head is used for each individual side of the disk.

Figure 2 shows sectors and tracks on a disk surface.

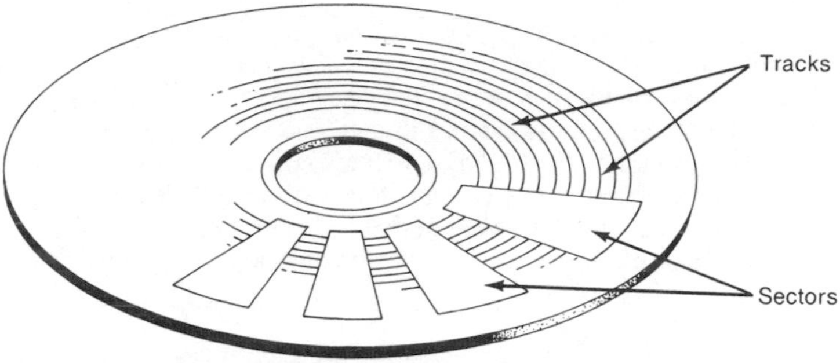

Fig. 2. Disk surface with sectors and tracks.

Hard disks can be purchased in many different capacities. Capacities range from 20M (megabytes) to 30M, 40M, 60M, and greater. Maximum capacities are greater than 300M.

Calculating Total Storage Capacity: Double-Sided Double-Density Floppy

To calculate the total storage capacity of a double-sided double-density floppy disk, multiply the following:

2 sides or surfaces
40 tracks
9 sectors per track
512 bytes per sector
368,640 total characters stored on the disk (360K)

Platters and Tracks

Hard disks have multiple rigid disks coated with iron oxide. Each disk is referred to as a platter. Each platter has two surfaces, as does a floppy disk. Two (or more depending on capacity) platters are inside the hard disk. Data is stored on those surfaces in tracks and sectors, as discussed previously. The average 20-megabyte hard disk uses 610 tracks on a surface (one side of the disk). Each track has more than 9 sectors, depending on the type of recording performed by the controller card, as explained later in this section. Standard XT and AT hard disks have 17 sectors per track. Each sector stores 512 characters (this is true for all sectors).

What Is a Cylinder?

Each platter has corresponding tracks on either side of the platter. Because more than one platter is in a hard disk, each platter has tracks that "line up" with the tracks on the other platter(s). This "lineup" of tracks is referred to as a cylinder. Each hard disk may vary as to the number of platters or cylinders that it may have. Most variations in capacity of hard disks are due to the number of platters and minor variations caused by the number of cylinders.

Calculating Total Storage Capacity: Hard Disk

To calculate the total storage capacity of a hard disk, multiply the following:

> 4 heads = 2 platters times 2 surfaces or sides
> 610 tracks
> 17 sectors per track
> 512 bytes per sector
> _____
> 21,237,760 total characters stored on the disk (20M)

Understanding your hard disk's geometry—the number of heads and cylinders—is important for the installation process. The hard disk geometry must be matched exactly to the number of heads and cylinders described in the computer's or disk controller's Read-Only Memory (ROM) for the disk to function properly. Performance also varies for different hard disks and controller combinations, as discussed later.

Hard Disk Speed

One of the principal benefits of using a hard disk is the speed of accessing data. What makes the hard disk so much faster than a floppy disk? The greatest contributor to the fast performance of a hard disk is its speed of rotation. LP phonograph records rotate at 33 1/3 RPM. Floppy disks rotate at 300 RPM (as do compact disks) but only while the drive light is on. When you retrieve information from a floppy, the drive must first rotate up to a speed of 300 RPM before the read/write head can be positioned over a specific area of the disk so data can be read.

A hard disk rotates at 3,600 RPM. It never stops unless the power is turned off. Consequently, when information is requested from the hard disk, the disk is already up to speed; only the read/write heads need to be positioned over the data to begin reading it into your computer. DOS causes the hard disk to read the directory information first to see where the data is stored on your disk. Once this process is complete, the heads are moved to a location where the data can be read into the computer.

Seek and Transfer Time

Because hard disk platters are continually rotating, the performance of each disk varies according to its seek time. Seek time is the amount of time necessary to move the read/write heads from cylinder to cylinder. The first XT hard disk had an average seek time of between 80 and 100 milliseconds (ms). The first AT hard disks reduced the average seek time to around 30 ms.

Today, average, low-cost drives that use a stepper motor to move the head from track to track provide an average seek time of about 65 ms. Stepper motor mechanisms work in fixed positions to which the head moves. High-performance full-height drives with voice coil head mechanisms for head movement can have average seek times of less than 20 ms. (Voice coil drives move the read/write heads by using coils of wire and a magnet.) Voice coil mechanisms work on the principle of electromagnetism—the same as an audio speaker. The speaker moves less with less sound or magnetic force and moves more with more sound or magnetic force.

Purchasing a hard disk with a quicker head seek time is the only way to get a hard disk to transfer information faster.

A list of some hard disk seek times follows:

Typical Disk Seek Times

XT Original	10M	100 ms
Seagate	20M	65 ms
Rodime	33M	57 ms
AT Original	20M	30 ms
Priam	60M	22 ms
Maxtor	140M	19 ms
Miniscribe	330M	17 ms

Hard Disk Controllers

Hard disk controllers must be capable of doing two things: transferring data from the system to the hard disk, and storing and reading that data from the hard disk. Various types of controller cards are available and use different methods to store data on the disk. The type of controller you choose will greatly affect the speed at which your data is transferred to and from your hard disk.

Types of Hard Disk Controllers

Basically three types of hard disk controllers are available: the Seagate ST-506/412 interface, Enhanced Small Device Interface (ESDI), and Small Computer Systems Interface (SCSI).

The ST-506/412 is the oldest, the least expensive, and probably the most common of the three controllers, especially for XTs.

The ESDI (despite the spelling, pronounced "Ed-zee"), becoming more common, is used in some of the faster higher-end 80286 and 80386 systems with hard disks greater than 70M. The ESDI is quickly becoming the new standard controller. It supports a 1 to 1 interleave, which provides superior performance.

SCSI (pronounced "Scuzzy") controllers are ideal when you want to attach ("daisy chain") several devices or other SCSI devices. SCSI's real claim to fame was the

Macintosh from Apple Computer Corp. Because of its ease of expandability, however, SCSI is becoming more used in the IBM and compatible world.

Data Storage Encoding Schemes

In addition to choosing one of the three types of hard disk controllers to transfer data to your hard disk, you may also choose an encoding scheme to determine the way your data is stored on your hard disk.

Two encoding schemes are commonly used with hard disks: Modified Frequency Modulation (MFM) and Run Length Limited (RLL). MFM is the older of the two.

MFM

A standard hard disk controller uses an encoding scheme called Modified Frequency Modulation (MFM). If you choose to use MFM, data will be stored evenly on a hard disk platter. MFM generally specifies that there will be 17 sectors per track and 512 bytes per sector.

RLL

A newer type of hard disk controller, using a more efficient type of encoding scheme, is capable of storing even more data on the same size disk. Run Length Limited (RLL) controllers turn a 20M hard disk into a 30M hard disk by creating 25 or 26 sectors per track. Multiply the following to see how RLL varies from MFM:

> 4 heads = 2 platters times 2 surfaces or sides
> 610 tracks
> 25 sectors per track
> 512 bytes per sector
>
> 31,232,000 total characters stored on the disk (30M)

Compare these calculations with those in the previous example involving a 20M hard disk. Notice that the number of tracks is the same, and the amount of data per sector is the same. The increase in storage comes from the number of sectors per track.

Many COMPAQ high-capacity hard disks use RLL controllers. *Warning:* An RLL controller should be used

only with a disk certified to function with that RLL
controller. Otherwise, the disk may lose data after it is in
use for a certain period of time. The high-capacity
COMPAQ portable hard disks use Extended Run Length
Limited (ERLL) controllers to extract greater storage
capacity from a single disk. These controllers store 33
sectors per track.

Interleave Factors

When a disk drive reads (or writes) a sector from the
disk, the drive must pass the data in that sector to the
hard disk controller. The controller then transfers the
data into the RAM of your computer. RAM is an area of
the computer used to store information in progress, prior
to being stored on disk. When the data transfer is
complete, the head can read/write again. During this data
transfer process, no more data can be read from the disk,
and the disk platter continues to rotate at a high speed.

Because the disk spins faster than the head can read the
sectors on that disk and transfer the data to RAM, the
controller must wait as the disk spins until the next
sector comes under the read/write head. At this pace,
many revolutions of the disk are needed to read adjacent
sectors. Because the sectors should not be read out of
order, numbering the sectors out of order is more
efficient. The new numbering takes into account just
how fast your particular controller works. This new
numbering scheme is called interleaving.

An interleave ratio of 4 to 1 means that the next
numbered sector is physically 4 sectors away from the
preceding one. For example, the sequential tracks at 4 to
1 are 0, 13, 9, 5, 1, 14, 10, 6, 2, 15, 11, 7, 3, 16, 12, 8, 4.
The result is that 4 sectors are read per revolution
instead of only 1 sector. A 4 to 1 interleave ratio is not
ideal for all systems. The correct interleave for any
system depends primarily on the controller and the speed
of your system.

Default interleave factors for XTs are 6 to 1 and for ATs
are 3 to 1. These are not optimal settings. You often can
improve the data transfer performance by 10 to 20
percent for XTs and ATs by reducing the interleave to 5
to 1 and 2 to 1, respectively.

Warning: If the interleave is reduced to the point where
the disk must wait an entire rotation for the sector to
reach the read/write heads, abysmally slow performance
will result.

Interleave Controller Programs

The optimum interleave for each hard disk and
controller combination is determined by programs that
test various interleave factors on the disk drive. These
programs perform the tests on a cylinder containing no
data. Two such commercial programs are Mace Utilities'
Hoptimum and Steve Gibson's Spin Test. Hard disk
performance is measured with the Coretest program by
Core International, Inc., a vendor of high-performance
disk drives.

Once the optimum interleave factor is determined, write
down that information for later use. The interleave can
only be set when you perform a physical format on the
hard disk.

PS/2 Model 50, 50 Z, and 60 systems have hard disk
controllers that buffer an entire track when reading a
disk. Buffering removes the interleave factor as a
determinant of the systems' data transfer performance.
Similarly, new controllers for XTs and ATs perform
full-track buffering to improve data transfer
performance. Actually, the disk on the PS/2 Model 50
performs similarly to the early XT hard disk. The
average seek time is in the 80 millisecond range.
However, the full-track buffering of the disk controller
provides performance equivalent to that of an AT hard
disk. The PS/2 Model 80 uses an ESDI controller for its
hard disks. This controller provides seek time
performance similar to the ESDI controller used with the
Miniscribe 330M.

In setting up your hard disk, you must understand the
interleave factor and how it affects the performance of
the disk. Choosing the correct interleave factor for your
disk can be the difference between a PC that performs
poorly and a PC that produces exceptional results.

Forms of Hard Disks

Hard disks are available in different storage capacities
and are often rated by the amount of information they
can hold. Hard disks can contain millions of characters,
called bytes. One megabtye (1M) is equal to 1,048,576
bytes, or roughly one million bytes. Physical size varies
based on the hard disk's storage capacity.

The following types of hard disks are available:

Half-Height 5 1/4-Inch Drives

Half-height 5 1/4-inch drives are the most common hard
disks found today. Storage capacities vary from 20M
(20,971,520 characters) to more than 40M (41,943,040
characters).

Half-Height 3 1/2-Inch Drives

The new small size and light weight of the half-height
3 1/2-inch drives make these ideal for portable and small
footprint desktop PCs.

Full-Height 5 1/4-Inch Drives

When higher storage capacity and high performance are
needed, full-height 5 1/4-inch drives are the preferred
drives. Storage capacities for this type of hard drive start
at 60M and run upward to 300M or 400M. MS-DOS 3.3
or 4.0 is required for you to work with these higher
capacity drives.

Hard Disk Cards

A hard disk card is usually a 3 1/2-inch drive mounted
on its controller card. The benefit here is installation
convenience with low power consumption, making these
cards ideal for early PCs and portable PCs. Early PCs'
and portable PCs' power supplies did not produce as
much power as they do today; early power supplies
produced 63.5 watts, and today's power supplies produce
192 watts of power.

Bernoulli Boxes

Some drives are equipped with removable media. Such drives are ideal for special applications requiring data transportability and security, because they can be removed from the system and locked up.

The Bernoulli Box is one type of drive with removable media. Bernoulli Boxes provide storage capacity and performance similar to that of hard disks. Bernoulli Box cartridges are floppy disks that operate on the Bernoulli principle that the air between the read/write head and the floppy disk moves faster than the air over the floppy itself, causing the floppy to bulge up slightly and move close to the read/write head. This principle provides excellent storage performance and reliable operation for removable media disks.

A Bernoulli Box cartridge looks like a normal 3 1/2-inch disk that has grown to 5 1/4 inches. It stores 10M to 40M of data per cartridge. The Bernoulli Boxes use a Small Computer Systems Interface (SCSI) adapter, which is faster than the standard ST412/506 interface used by many hard disks. The disks inside Bernoulli Box cartridges rotate continuously at 1,850 RPM, requiring no start time like a standard floppy disk. These disks are excellent for archiving data and storing confidential data that must be locked up.

WORM Drives

Another type of removable media is the Write Once Read Many (WORM) drive. WORM drives are optical drives (similar to compact disks) that use lasers to write permanently and later read platters storing several hundred million characters on a single disk. A WORM drive's performance is not as fast as today's average hard disk, but as the technology improves, expect WORM drives to be as fast as most hard disks on the market.

The real benefit of WORM drives is that data, once written, cannot be destroyed. When backing up regular hard disks, you may accidentally write new bad data over older good data, therefore destroying the older data. Because all data written to a WORM drive is permanently written to the drive, the WORM drive is beneficial for archiving data that must be kept permanently.

SETTING UP YOUR HARD DISK

Steps for Setting Up Your Hard Disk

Hard disk setup involves the following steps:

1. Physical installation of the disk drive

2. Physical (low-level) formatting of the drive (which includes marking defective portions of the disk and selecting the interleave factor)

3. Partitioning of the drive using FDISK

4. Formatting of the drive for DOS (to set up the FAT and directory and install the operating system)

Once you complete these steps, you can tune the disk to your specific computer system by specifying the number of open files, number of buffers, file control blocks, cache memory, and RAM disks.

Installation Differences

Installation procedures for hard disks vary. In many cases, the same physical drive may be installed in an XT computer as in an AT computer, but due to the drive controller combination, the installation procedure will differ.

XT Hard Disk Installation

XT computers have the drive geometry (the number of heads and cylinders) stored in Read-Only Memory (ROM) on the hard disk controller card. Typically, an XT controller works with four disk types: two 10M and two 20M geometries. Therefore, XTs support fewer drive types than ATs. The drive and controller card are bought as a kit. Once installed, the drive and controller should not be separated. If you try swapping controller XT cards with different drives, the new combination may not work unless the drive is reformatted.

AT Hard Disk Installation

ATs have the drive geometry stored in their ROM BIOS (Read-Only Memory Basic Input/Output System) on the system board rather than on the hard disk controller card. Each hard disk specification in ROM BIOS (that is, how many heads, platters, and cylinders each disk has) is given a *type*. The Setup program prompts you to enter your hard disk type. The drive types vary from 24 types in early ATs to 47 types in new ATs and clones. Be careful when installing drives in clones because the drive types often do not exactly match those in IBM's AT BIOS ROM. The Seagate 4096 80M drive is a type 35 on some ATs, for example, but a type 12 on the Packard Bell 386/20.

The initial drive preparation for XTs is performed with the use of ROM on the controller board, but the AT advanced diagnostics generally perform the primary formatting of the AT disk drive. ESDI and RLL controllers are similar to XT controllers in that they also have the primary formatting performed by setup software in ROM on the controller board. Further information on drive installation is discussed in the next section, "Hardware Installation."

Hardware Installation

This section provides general hardware installation instructions for mounting one or two internal hard disks in a PC, XT, AT, or clone system. Information provided by your system dealer describes more precisely the details for your disk drive.

Prior to placing the hard disk in the computer, look on the disk for a sheet containing the "Bad Track List." This is a list of known problem areas on the disk. Make a copy of the list of these problem areas for reference when you perform the physical format on the hard disk.

Hard Disk Connections

Following are the necessary hard disk connections for the first part of the hardware installation procedure:

- The power connector, which is a four-conductor cable. There is one power cable for each disk drive.

- The control cable, which is a 34-conductor ribbon cable. One control cable can handle both disk drives.

- The data cable, which is a 20-conductor ribbon cable. A single data cable is required for each disk drive.

- Drive select jumpers. There is generally a bank of four to eight pins on each disk drive.

Figure 3 shows the power, control cable, and data cable connections for some of the more common Seagate disk drives.

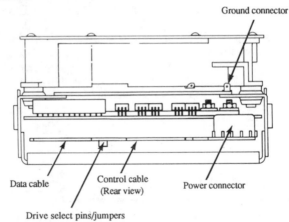

Fig. 3. Connection locations.

Note: The connectors shown in figure 3 may be in different locations on other disk drives.

The key slot identifies the pin 1 side of the connector toward which the colored edge (also pin 1) of the cable must be facing.

The power cable connector is keyed to ensure proper insertion. A separate power cable is connected to each hard disk. No differences exist between power cables for hard disk C and hard disk D.

You can use several types of control cables to connect the hard disk to the controller. You need to determine which of the cables listed next matches the cable you are using. The type of cable you are using determines where the drive select jumper should be on the hard disk. The pin nearest to the notch on the edge connector is pin 1; pin 1 is always connected to pin 1.

Identifying the Proper Cable

A 34-conductor cable with only one edge connector is designed for a system that has only one hard disk. The drive select jumper (a set of jumper pins used to select the drive address—where the data is to be channeled—such as C or D) must be on the first pair of jumper pins, and a terminating resistor (an integrated circuit used on the hard disk at the end of the signal cable) should be installed on the drive.

A 34-conductor cable with two edge connectors—one in the middle of the cable and one on the end of the cable— is designed for use in systems that have two hard disks, although it can be used in single hard disk systems as well. Often, some of the conductors near one connector will be twisted (see fig. 4). This twist allows both drive select pins to be set identically. The twisted wires cause the drives to be addressed individually rather than as the same drive. When a cable with a twist is used on a single hard disk system, the single hard disk should be connected at the end of the cable.

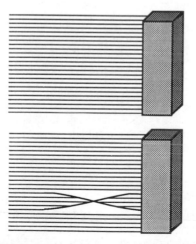

Fig. 4. Top cable with no twist. Bottom cable with a twist.

The cables for hard disk and floppy disk drives are similar in appearance, but they have one important distinction:

- The floppy drive cable has the twisted wires *nearest to* the edge with the colored wire—the pin 1 side.

- The hard disk cable has the twisted wires *farthest from* the edge with the colored wire—the pin 1 side.

Connecting the Drive Select Jumper

The drive select jumper is a set of pins used to differentiate each hard disk on your computer. Without drive select jumpers, all hard disks attached to your system would activate at the same time. With drive select jumpers, each hard disk attached to a computer has its own identity.

The basic rules for connecting the drive select jumper follow:

- Control cables with a single hard disk connector indicate that the drive select jumper should be on the first pair of jumper pins.

- Control cables with connectors for two hard disks and wires 25-29 twisted between the middle and the end hard drive connectors indicate that *both hard disks* should have the drive select jumper connected to the second pair of jumper pins.

- Control cables with connectors for two hard disks and no twisted wires indicate that the drive select jumper should be on the first pair of pins for drive C and on the second pair of pins for drive D.

When the data cable is improperly installed, the error message `Error Reading Fixed Disk` appears when you boot your hard disk. Improperly reversing the connectors on the data cables is easy (for example, connecting pin 1 to pin 20). The data cables are the narrow (20-conductor) ribbon cables.

Typical Controller Layout

The controller shown in figure 5 is a typical XT type of controller. Hard disk controllers may have a different layout of components, but the connectors should be as shown in the figure. The typical XT hard disk controller has three connectors. These connectors may be laid out in a horizontal or vertical fashion on the side of the controller farthest from the metal connector fastening it to the computer.

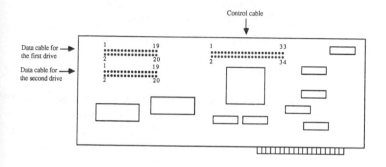

Fig. 5. XT hard drive controller.

The typical AT hard disk controller has four connectors—three for the hard disks and one for the floppy drives. They are laid out in a vertical fashion near the center of the control board. Figure 6 shows the four horizontal connectors. The right-most connector is for the floppy controller cable. It handles both control functions and data transfer for the floppy drives. The next connector is the control cable for the hard disks. To its left is the connector for the data cable for drive C, and the left-most connector is the data cable for drive D. Generally, pin 1 on the controller is located at the top of the board for all connectors on the AT controller.

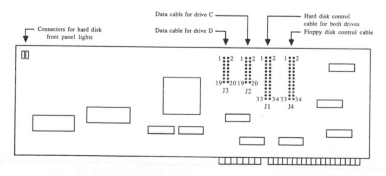

Fig. 6. AT 16-bit controller with four connectors.

The controller shown in figure 6 is typical of AT 16-bit
controllers. Your controller may have a different layout
of components, but it should have the connectors shown.

Identifying Pin 1 on a Cable

Pin 1 on a cable is indicated by the following:

- A triangular pointer on the connector, the colored
  wire on one side of the ribbon cable

- A number 1-2, 20, or 33-34 on the face of the
  connector

- An extra notch offset on one side of the connector

- A plastic block inside a hole in the connector that
  mates with a missing pin on the controller board
  (preventing incorrect insertion)

Identifying Pin 1 on the Controller

Use one of the following methods to identify pin 1 on
the controller:

- The number 1, 2, 20, 33, or 34 is printed on the card
  near one end of the row of pins. Note that pins 20,
  33, and 34 are at the end of the connector opposite
  pin 1. Remember that pin 1 must be connected to
  pin 1.

- A square solder pad is located on the back side of
  the controller board, into which the connector pins
  are soldered. All the connector pins except pin 1
  have round pads. Pin 1 has the only square pad.

Connecting the Cables

The connector at the end of the control cable is
connected to the first hard disk in the computer. When
the cable does have a twist, connect the drive select
jumper to the second pair of jumper pins and leave the
terminating resistor in the disk drive.

The connector in the middle of the cable is for the
second hard disk in the computer. Again, place the drive
select jumper on the second pair of jumper pins but
remove the terminating resistor from the disk drive.

When the cable does not have twisted wires, drive 1
(drive C) must have the drive select jumper connected to
the first pair of jumper pins.

The objective is to connect pin 1 on the cable to pin 1 on
the controller. In order for the control and data cables to
be connected properly to the hard disk controller, pin 1
must be located on the cable as well as on the controller.
Cables are often designed to connect to the controller or
hard disk in only one way. This type of cable is called a
"keyed" cable and ensures that cables are connected
properly.

When the cables are connected properly, the control
cable is used to activate or address drive C, for example.
The correct information travels through the control cable
to activate drive C. The information that you request
(when you read a file, for example) travels through the
data cable.

Completing the Hardware Installation

Connect the controller cable to one or both hard disks.
Next, connect the smaller ribbon cables to the data
connectors for each hard disk. Be sure to connect data
cables to the correct controller connections for drive C
or drive D.

Common Installation Errors

When users install hard disks, they often improperly
install the drive select jumper. If the drive select jumper
is not installed properly, you get the error message `No
Fixed Disks Present` when you boot your hard
disk. You can correct this error by simply changing the
jumper location to the next position.

A common mistake users make when installing data
cables is connecting drive C's cable to the drive D
connector on the controller. When there are two hard
disks, each hard disk needs one data cable installed.

Another common mistake users make is installing the
control cable for the hard disk backward—for example,
connecting pin 1 to pin 34 by reversing the connectors.
This error is easy to spot because the light for the hard
disk comes on and stays on permanently when the
system is powered on. The normal sequence for lights on

your system is as follows: the hard disk light briefly flashes after the system is powered up, the floppy disk light flashes, and finally, the hard disk light briefly flashes as the computer boots from the hard disk.

Software Installation

What Is Involved in Software Setup?

Software setup varies from system to system and hard disk to hard disk. Software setup first requires specifying the proper drive geometry (the number of heads and cylinders) to the hard disk controller or the AT system. With XT controllers, the drive geometry is often determined by jumpers on the controller board. The controller board documentation describes the proper setting for those jumpers for your specific disk drive. On the AT, you need to have the drive type number specified by the disk manufacturer (sometimes it is stated on the label on the disk drive) or consult the listing of typical drive types in table 1, which lists some of the more common nonstandard disk drives with their IBM PC AT "TYPE" codes.

Nonstandard disk drives are those not specifically provided for in the ROM BIOS of your particular computer.

Once drive geometry is determined, software installation begins. On PCs and XTs, the primary formatting is performed by the controller card and the DOS DEBUG program.

The Setup Program

Running the setup program is a simple process. For example, the IBM AT Setup program is easy to use. Just place the disk Diagnostics for IBM Personal Computer AT into drive A and boot the computer. When the following menu appears, choose option 4 to set up the computer:

```
The IBM Personal Computer
DIAGNOSTICS
Version 2.02
```

```
         (C) Copyright IBM Corp.
              1981, 1985

         SELECT AN OPTION
         0 - SYSTEM CHECKOUT
         1 - FORMAT DISKETTE
         2 - COPY DISKETTE
         3 - PREPARE SYSTEM FOR MOVING
         4 - SETUP
         9 - END DIAGNOSTICS
         SELECT THE ACTION DESIRED
         ? 4
```

Answering Setup Questions

As Setup runs, you must enter the correct date and time

Table 1
Common AT Types of Disk Drives

MANUFACTURER/MODEL	CAPACITY	TYPE(PC-AT)	NO.OF CYL	NO.OF HEADS	SEC/TRACK
CONTROL DATA 94155-30	17.7 MB	NONE	697	3	17
CONTROL DATA 94155-36	29.6 MB	6	697	5	17
CONTROL DATA 94155-38	31.1 MB	8	733	5	17
CONTROL DATA 94155-48	39.3 MB	11	925	5	17
CONTROL DATA 94205	42.0 MB	11	989	5	17
CONTROL DATA 94155-67	55.0 MB	12	925	7	17
CONTROL DATA 94155-86	70.7 MB	12	925	9	17
FUJITSU M2242AS	44.8 MB	14	754	7	17
FUJITSU M2243AS	70.5 MB	14	754	11	17
HITACHI DK511-5	42.4 MB	6	714	7	17
HITACHI DK511-8	69.9 MB	14	823	10	17
MAXTOR XT-1065	54.6 MB	12	918	7	17
MAXTOR XT-1085	69.6 MB	12	1024	8	17
MAXTOR XT-1105	85.8 MB	12	918	11	17
MAXTOR XT-1140	117.0 MB	9	918	15	17
MAXTOR XT-2190	130.6 MB	9	1024	15	17
MICROPOLIS 1324	52.2 MB	5	1024	6	17
MICROPOLIS 1325	69.6 MB	4	1024	8	17
MINISCRIBE 6085	69.6 MB	4	1024	8	17
MINISCRIBE 9080e	330.0 MB	9	1224	1*	34
NEWBURY DATA 1065	54.6 MB	12	918	7	17
NEWBURY DATA 1085	69.6 MB	12	1024	8	17
NEWBURY DATA 1105	85.8 MB	12	918	11	17
NEWBURY DATA 1140	117.0 MB	9	918	15	17
NEWBURY DATA 2190	130.6 MB	9	1024	15	17
NEC D5146	41.8 MB	6	615	8	17
PRIAM	41.7 MB	11	981	5	17
PRIAM	58.4 MB	12	981	7	17
SEAGATE ST213	10.5 MB	NONE	615	2	17
SEAGATE ST225	20.9 MB	2	615	4	17
SEAGATE ST238	20.9 MB	6	615	4	17
SEAGATE ST251	41.8 MB	3	820	6	17
SEAGATE ST277	61.0 MB	3 (RLL)	820	6	25
SEAGATE ST4026	20.9 MB	2	615	4	17
SEAGATE ST4038	31.1 MB	8	733	5	17
SEAGATE ST4051	41.5 MB	11	977	5	17
SEAGATE ST4096	78.3 MB	12	1024	9	17
TANDON TM755	41.7 MB	11	980	5	17
TOSHIBA MK53	35.3 MB	8	830	5	17
TOSHIBA MK54	49.4 MB	14	830	7	17
TOSHIBA MK56	70.6 MB	14	830	10	17
VERTEX V170	58.7 MB	12	987	7	17
VERTEX V185	60.9 MB	12	1024	7	17

*Drive type 1 is used by ESDI controllers because
they read the drive type number from the hard disk
itself.

for the battery-backed-up clock. Then Setup displays a list of options:

```
The following options have been
set:

Diskette Drive A - High Capacity
(1.2Mb)
Diskette Drive B - Not Installed
Fixed Disk Drive C - Type 2
Fixed Disk Drive D - Not Installed
Base memory size - 640Kb
Expansion memory size - 0Kb
Primary display is:
   - Color Display (80 columns)

Are these options correct (Y/N)
?
```

If any of the options are incorrect, enter **N** and change your selection(s). Notice that the Setup program determined that there is only one fixed disk and it is of type 2.

If the answers are correct, answer **Y** and press Enter. You are prompted to press Enter again. The setup is saved in memory backed up by the battery, and the computer resets. The computer will remember its configuration each time you start it.

Software Installation Errors

If the wrong drive type is specified, your disk will not operate properly. Your disk may be specified to have less storage capacity than it actually has, or your disk may become damaged by trying to read more cylinders than actually exist on the disk. To correct these errors rerun Setup and choose the correct type of hard disk.

Examining the PS/2 Setup Program

To run the setup program for a PS/2 system, you must boot the Reference disk distributed with each computer. The setup for a PS/2 system is much simpler than the setup for an AT. When you add a new device such as a memory board to your PS/2 computer, reboot from the Reference disk. The setup program will run automatically after you press PgDn, **Y**, and Enter twice, when prompted. This process is known as the Autoconfiguration.

Performing a Physical Format

You must perform a physical format to test the hard disk and flag any errors (also known as bad tracks) to be avoided. A physical format can be accomplished with a program such as the advanced diagnostics program provided by the manufacturer (such as IBM's Advanced Diagnostics) or a program such as HFORMAT provided by Paul Mace.

You may want to run a program to test the optimum interleave factor prior to performing a physical format. This program will evaluate various interleave factors and select the most appropriate for your needs.

Before you perform the physical format, remember that you must identify your type of hard disk in order to enter the setup. You must know the bad tracks on that hard disk as well. Each hard disk usually comes with a manufacturer's list of known bad tracks. Flag these tracks so they will not be used by designating them as bad tracks in the setup procedure.

PC and XT Physical Format

The procedure is to boot your system from a floppy and run DEBUG by entering **DEBUG**. This procedures takes you to the DEBUG prompt:

```
A:\ >DEBUG
-
```

Then enter **G=C800:5**. This sequence runs the hard disk setup program in the ROM on the controller board. Your screen displays the following:

```
A:\ >DEBUG
-G=C800:5
```

Some controllers use different starting locations for the setup ROM program. If C800:5 does not work, you have two alternatives: C800:6 and C800:ccc.

AT Physical Format

AT setup requires running a special program that comes with your computer. You must first specify the correct drive type by running the Setup program. You can use other programs—for example, Paul Mace's

HOPTIMUM or HFORMAT—to change the hard disk
interleave factor and perform the physical (low-level)
format of the   hard disk.

Once you have set the disk drive interleave and
performed the primary format, you can proceed to
partitioning your hard disk with FDISK.

The Partitioning Process

A hard disk must be partitioned before an operating
system, such as DOS, can be placed on it. If you are
using DOS 3.3 or earlier, the maximum partition size is
32M. Therefore, if your hard disk is larger than 32M,
you must create more than one partition. Also, if you use
more than one operating system, you will have to create
more than one partition on your hard disk. Each
operating system requires its own paritition.

How DOS Divides Hard Disks

When reading the hard disk, DOS searches through the
master boot record, the directory, and the File Allocation
Table (FAT). The partitioning process sets up master
boot records for each disk drive partition. The DOS
FDISK program performs the partitioning. The
FORMAT command creates the master or root directory
and the FAT.

How FDISK Works

First, FDISK asks you to set a *primary* DOS partition
and specify the number of cylinders in that partition (see
table 1 on page 23 for the number of cylinders for your
type of hard disk). Once the partition is established,
FDISK assigns that drive a logical drive letter (usually
C). Because DOS versions up through 3.3 cannot work
with a drive larger than 32M and many hard disks are
larger than 32M, you may not be able to partition your
entire hard disk. To avoid losing the additional space,
you can use DOS 3.3's FDISK to set up an *extended*
partition. The extended partition is assigned to the
remaining disk space where the primary partition left off
and continues to the end of the disk. FDISK must know
the starting cylinder and the number of cylinders to

include in a partition. FDISK always keeps you apprised of total cylinders and how many have been assigned.

Once the extended partition is defined, FDISK requests that logical drive letters be assigned to the extended partition. The number of cylinders for that drive letter is specified, giving the logical drive its storage capacity. If the extended partition is greater than 32M, a second logical drive is assigned, then a third, and so on, until all the extended partition is in use.

Remember that the *physical* drive is the tangible hard drive you purchased for your computer. You may have one *physical* drive, but that drive may be partitioned into two *logical* drives—drives C and D, for example.

COMPAQ's DOS 3.31 and IBM's DOS 4.0 are slightly different. They allow partitions greater than 32M. When you're using these versions of DOS, FDISK may assign the entire drive as the primary partition, and the entire disk will become drive C.

Partitioning Strategies

When you create the primary DOS partition, FDISK asks whether you want to use the maximum size for the DOS partition and to make this partition active. The answer to this question depends on the version of DOS you use and your hard disk size. If you have DOS 3.3, answering **Y** will partition up to 32M of your hard disk. With DOS 3.31 or later versions, answering **Y** will assign your entire hard disk as the primary partition. Answering **N** will allow you to determine the size you want for your primary partition.

Because some programs you use (normally utilities) may not work with partitions greater than 32M, you may want to keep your primary partition within the 32M limit. Software packages that do not work properly with partitions larger than 32M include early versions of Norton Utilities, PC Tools, and Mace Utilities. Current versions of these programs are not limited in this way.

Most programs that use DOS and do not work directly with the hard disk can use partition sizes greater than 32M. However, because you may have some programs that require the original DOS FAT size, the best approach is to set up large hard disks with a primary

partition equal to 32M or less. You may choose the size
of the remaining partitions.

Partitioning Using FDISK

To use FDISK, you must first boot your computer with
your DOS disk. Once you have entered the date and
time, enter **FDISK** at the A> prompt.

Note: The FDISK screens vary with different versions of
PC DOS and MS-DOS.

The FDISK Main Menu

In the partitioning process, the first FDISK menu
identifies the disk drive with which you are working.
This drive may be identified as drive 1 or drive 2. Then
you are asked to choose from among 4 options. Here is a
sample screen displayed at this point:

```
FDISK Options

Current Fixed Disk Drive:  1

Choose one of the following:

1. Create DOS partition
2. Change Active Partition
3. Delete DOS partition
4. Display Partition Information

Enter choice:  [1]

Press ESC to return to DOS
```

If you have additional hard disk drives, another choice
appears:

```
5. Select next fixed disk drive
```

Choose option 1, Create DOS partition. Next
you are asked to create a primary or extended DOS
partition, as shown by the following screen :

```
Create DOS Partition

Current Fixed Disk Drive:  1

1. Create Primary DOS partition
2. Create Extended DOS partition
3. Create logical DOS drive(s) in
   the Extended DOS partition
```

```
Enter choice:  [1]

Press ESC to return to FDISK
Options
```

Once you assign your primary partition, you see the
following message:

```
System will now restart

Insert DOS diskette in drive A:
Press any key when ready...
```

If your primary partition is less than the entire size of
your hard disk, you should assign an extended partition.
Following is the screen you should use to define your
extended partition:

```
   Create Extended DOS Partition

Current Fixed Disk Drive: 1

Partition   C: 1
Status A
Type  PRI DOS
Size in Mbytes  30
Percentage of Disk Used  30%

Total disk space is 100 Mbytes
(1 Mbyte = 1048576 bytes)

Enter partition size in Mbytes or
percent of disk space (%) to create
an Extended DOS Partition.....[ 70]

Press ESC to return to FDISK
Options
```

Note: DOS 3.3 requests the number of cylinders to
assign to each partition instead of the percentage of the
hard disk to assign to each cylinder. Cylinders begin
with 0. A hard disk with 605 cylinders will number them
0 through 604.

Once the extended partition is defined, it must be
subdivided into logical drives. The logical drive
assignments involve assigning drive letters to your
extended partition. For DOS 3.3, each drive letter may
occupy 32M. Therefore, a 70M hard disk can be divided
into a primary partition of 32M, drive C, and a 38M
extended partition. The extended partition can be split

between two logical drives—drive D of 20M and drive
E of 18M, for example.

Using Multiple Logical Partitions

Having multiple logical partitions restricts the drive
heads to specific sets of cylinders and consequently can
improve performance for programs always accessing the
disk (for example, dBASE and WordPerfect). Within the
logical drive, the seek time is lessened slightly because
the heads only need to move among a few cylinders. For
example, a drive with 318M of storage capacity may be
partitioned by DOS 4.0 into a 32M drive and a 286M
logical drive. Searches through many files in the
extended DOS 286M partition are convenient, but these
searches are noticeably slower than if the extended
partition was subdivided into several smaller drives.

Specifying Logical Drives

FDISK prompts you to specify logical drives by
presenting you with the following screen:

```
Create Logical DOS Drive(s) in the
Extended DOS Partition

No logical drives defined.

Total Extended DOS Partition size
is 70 Mbytes (1 Mbyte = 1048576
bytes)  Maximum space available for
logical drive is 70 Mbytes (70%)

Enter logical drive size in Mbytes
or percent of disk space (%)..[ 70]

Press ESC to return to FDISK
Options
```

Note: Again, your version of FDISK may ask for the
number of cylinders rather than a percentage.

Designating the Active Partition

Once the logical partitions are specified in the extended
DOS partition, you must designate one partition as
active. The active partition becomes the partition from
which DOS boots. Normally, the primary partition is the
active partition. The active partition menu follows:

```
    Set Active Partition

Current Fixed Disk Drive: 1

Partition        C:  1    2
Status
Type            PRI DOS   EXT DOS
Size in Mbytes    30        70
Percentage of Disk Used  30%   70%

Total disk space is 100 Mbytes (1
Mbyte = 1048576 bytes)

Enter the number of the partition
you want to make active:[1]

Press ESC to return to FDISK
Options
```

Displaying Partition Information

After the partitioning is complete, the logical drives are specified, and DOS is rebooted, you can display the partition information. For example, the following screen displays this message:

```
    Display Partition Information

Current Fixed Disk Drive: 1

Partition        C:  1    2
Status
Type            PRI DOS   EXT DOS
Size in Mbytes    30        70
Percentage of Disk Used  30%   70%

Total disk space is 100 Mbytes (1
Mbyte = 1048576 bytes)

The Extended DOS Partition contains
Logical DOS Drives.
Do you want to display the logical
drive information (Y/N)...?[Y]

Press ESC to return to FDISK
Options
```

Examining Partition Differences

Differences between DOS 4.0 and earlier versions are shown by this partition display from DOS 3.3:

```
    Display Partition Information
Current Fixed Disk Drive: 1

Partition      C:  1    2
Status
Type              PRI DOS    EXT DOS
Start                0       244
End                243       746
Size               244       503

Total disk space is 747 cylinders.

The Extended DOS partition contains
logical DOS drives. Do you want to
display logical drive information?
[Y]
```

Viewing the logical drives yields the following screen:

```
Display Logical DOS Drive
Information

Drv Start End  Size
D:  244    746  503

Press ESC to return to FDISK
Options
```

Formatting Your Hard Disk

Performing a High-Level Format

The next step is to high-level (logical) format your hard disk by using the DOS FORMAT command. Formatting the disk establishes the directory and FAT for the drive partitions.

FORMAT /S

Format the active partition and place the necessary system files in it by using the following command:

FORMAT C: /S

This command formats drive C. The /S option places IBMBIO.COM and IBMDOS.COM as the first two files on the disk. These files are marked as system, read-only, and hidden—you cannot view them with the DIR (Directory) command—and must be the first files on the disk. FORMAT also copies COMMAND.COM to the root directory. Following is the screen that appears after you enter this comand:

```
E:\ >FORMAT C: /S
Warning! The data on drive C: will
be destroyed.

Do you want to continue the format
(Y/N)? [y]

Press ENTER to begin formatting C:
Head:  4 Cylinder:  6
```

FORMAT

You must format each partition subsequently by using

FORMAT *d:*

where *d:* is the next physical or logical drive to format.

You receive no benefit by placing system files in partitions that are not the active or boot partitions.

When a hard disk is *reformatted* by DOS, the data is usually not lost. The only changes to the disk are the replacement of the old directory and FAT with a new empty directory and FAT. Programs such as Mace Utilities, Norton Utilities, and PC Tools can make copies of the directory and the FAT in a file stored on the hard disk. The file containing the directory and FAT should be updated often. In this manner, if the disk is accidentally reformatted, special recovery programs provided by each utility seek out those files and use them to replace the empty directory and FAT, restoring all lost data.

If you stop the reformatting before the process is complete, the directory and FAT have not been over-written and your data remains intact. To interrupt the formatting, use Ctrl-Break.

The Purpose of the FAT

The 32M limit for DOS partitions for DOS 3.3 and earlier versions was determined by the number of entries in the FAT and the amount of disk space referenced by each cluster. A cluster may be one or more sectors, depending on the disk size. It is the basic unit in which disk space is allocated. The FAT links the directory entries to the actual data on the hard disk by using these clusters. For 32M hard disks, the clusters are 4 sectors, or 2,048 characters. There is a maximum of 16,384 entries in the FAT. Because each entry represents 1 cluster, 16,384 entries times 2,048 characters per cluster gives a maximum partition size of 33,554,432, otherwise referred to as 32M. DOS 4.0 circumvents this limitation by making the number of sectors per cluster greater than 4.

Configuration Commands

The next step in the preparation process is to set up the CONFIG.SYS file that tells DOS how to configure your system.

The Purpose of a CONFIG.SYS File

The CONFIG.SYS file is merely a list of commands issued to load programs or change system parameters after both IBMBIO.COM and IBMDOS.COM have been loaded into RAM. CONFIG.SYS can be created with a simple line-editing program such as EDLIN, which comes with DOS.

A CONFIG.SYS file is often required by special system hardware such as a Local Area Network (LAN), scanner, or other special input/output devices attached to your computer. Software such as dBASE and WordPerfect may also require a CONFIG.SYS file because these programs do not work well with the standard DOS configuration defaults.

The CONFIG.SYS commands that change the operating parameters of the system follow.

BREAK

The BREAK command in the CONFIG.SYS file determines when DOS will check for Ctrl-Break, which aborts a running program. Occasionally, you may press Ctrl-Break, but the program will not stop. The reason is that Ctrl-Break is checked by DOS and not by the program itself. When a program is running, it often does not require services from DOS, or if for some unknown reason the program enters an endless loop, it may not request DOS services. In both cases, Ctrl-Break has no effect on DOS and, consequently, does not stop the program.

With the line

BREAK=OFF

Ctrl-Break is only accepted when the program is working with the keyboard, the screen, a printer, or an auxiliary device such as the serial port.

The line

BREAK=ON

in a CONFIG.SYS file tells DOS to check for Ctrl-Break before performing any DOS operation. This setting is the system default as well.

BUFFERS

A buffer is a portion of RAM that stores data temporarily while the data is being transferred from one device to another. The BUFFERS command checks this area of RAM for data before reading from or writing to the hard disk. Because RAM access time is 10 to 100 times faster than disk access time, specifying a large number of buffers can speed up disk operations and, consequently, the execution of programs when they access the hard disk. The drawback is that each buffer requires 528 (DOS 3.3) characters of RAM, making that RAM unavailable for programs. The default value for BUFFERS is 3.

In DOS 4.0 you also can specify look-ahead buffers with the BUFFERS command. A look-ahead buffer is 512 characters. These buffers allow DOS to read more sectors before processing any of the data read, which can speed up disk input and output. The default setting is 0, and the maximum setting is 8. When look-ahead buffers equal 3, DOS will read 3 sectors from disk. Later, if DOS requests a sector, it may already be in memory. The sector then can be transferred from the look-ahead buffer to the application program, thus speeding up disk access. Look-ahead buffers are not helpful for random unordered (nonsequential) reads and writes to disk because they can cause DOS to read extra sectors that will be discarded later as data from other areas of the disk are read into memory.

The syntax for BUFFERS through DOS 3.31 is

> **BUFFERS=***nn*

where *nn* is the number of disk buffers from 1 to 99.

The syntax for BUFFERS with DOS 4.0 and look-ahead buffers is

> **BUFFERS =***nn,m* **/X**

where *nn* is the number of disk buffers from 1 to 99 and *m* is the number of look-ahead buffers from 1 to 8. The default is 0. The /X option places BUFFERS in expanded memory.

If you use a database program, for example, you will be instructed to increase your BUFFER setting from 3 (the default) to 15, for example, by typing

> **BUFFERS=15**

in your CONFIG.SYS file. Experiment with BUFFERS to tune your computer's performance.

DEVICE

You can use the DEVICE command in your CONFIG.SYS file to add programs that handle special hardware functions to DOS. These programs are called device drivers. Two popular device drivers are VDISK.SYS and ANSI.SYS. Other device drivers are required for some Local Area Networks, scanner hardware, Bernoulli Box drives, nonstandard floppy drives, and so on. DOS already contains device drivers for standard input, output, printer, floppy disk, and hard disk functions.

The syntax for DEVICE is

> **DEVICE=***d:path\filename.ext*

where *d:path* is the path to the device driver and *filename.ext* is the device driver.

Specifying, for example,

DEVICE=C:\DOS\ANSI.SYS

installs the ANSI.SYS device driver software to provide
expanded standard input and output functions such as
redefining keys on the keyboard or setting custom screen
colors. Once your system is rebooted and ANSI.SYS is
installed, enter the following command:

prompt $e[1A$e[55C$d thhp $g

Your screen prompt changes. Instead of seeing C>, you
see the date and time on the right side of the screen and
the drive letter and current path on the left.

FCBS

The FCBS command specifies the number of File
Control Blocks that can be used concurrently by DOS.
You do not need to use this command unless your
application program specifically requests it in the
program's documentation or unless you initiate file
sharing by using the SHARE command. DOS Version
2.0 introduced the use of file handles, specified with the
FILES directive. FCBS has limited use now.

The syntax for FCBS is

FCBS=*x,y*

where *x* is the maximum number of File Control Blocks
a program can use at one time and *y* is the minimum
number of File Control Blocks that should remain open.
The default value is FCBS=4,0.

A line placed in CONFIG.SYS, for example, is

FCBS=16,8

The first number, 16, specifies the maximum number of
files opened by FCBS that DOS is permitted to keep
active (open) at one time. The second number, 8,
determines the number of files opened by FCBS that
cannot be closed by DOS. Note that these are the files
opened by FCBS—not just by DOS.

FILES

This parameter specifies the maximum number of files
that can be kept open simultaneously. The default value

is 8 files, and the maximum value is 255. Each increase in the number of open files above 8 adds from 48 (DOS 3.0 through 3.3) to 64 (DOS 4.0) bytes of RAM to the memory-resident portion of DOS. DOS provides 5 predefined files for standard input, standard output, error reports, auxiliary data, and printer data. Most programs, such as LAN programs, word processors, or database programs, require the number of active files to be larger than the default. If not enough files have been specified, your application program usually displays an error message such as `Too many files open`.

The syntax for FILES is

FILES=*nnn*

where *nnn* is a number from 8 to 255. An appropriate number for PCs connected to a LAN and using a database program is **FILES=25**.

LASTDRIVE

The LASTDRIVE command tells DOS the maximum number of disk drives that your system can use. This command may be used when a system has a very large disk partitioned into several smaller disks, when you are using a LAN, or when you use SUBST (Substitute) to give a path name a drive letter.

The syntax for LASTDRIVE is

LASTDRIVE=*d*

where *d* is the highest letter from A through Z that can be used as a drive. The LASTDRIVE default is E.

By specifying

LASTDRIVE=J

you may have drive designations from A through J.

SHELL

The SHELL command tells DOS where to find a command processor, if you choose to replace or relocate COMMAND.COM, so that it can be reloaded into RAM.

The syntax for SHELL is

SHELL=*d:path\filename.ext d:compath*\/**P**
/**E:***size*

where *d:path\filename.ext* is the drive, path, and name of
the command processor, *d:compath*\ is the path to the
command processor, /P keeps the command processor
permanent, and /E:*size* sets the size of the environment.
The environment is an area of memory that holds
information used by DOS.

If you decide to place COMMAND.COM in a
subdirectory called C:\DOS instead of in its default
location of the root directory, add this command to your
CONFIG.SYS file:

SHELL=C:\DOS\COMMAND.COM C:\DOS
/**P** /**E:512**

Notice that /E:512 sets your environment size to 512
bytes.

Note: If you indicated a different location for
COMMAND.COM or a different command processor in
your AUTOEXEC.BAT file, the SHELL statement in
your CONFIG.SYS file must agree with the COMSPEC
statement used with the SET command in your
AUTOEXEC.BAT file.

STACKS

Stacks process hardware interrupts by allowing DOS to
jump to a subroutine to perform a specific function and
then return to where DOS stopped processing. DOS
provides 9 stack frames with a size of 128 bytes for most
PCs. However, the early PC, XT, and Portable PC do
not provide stacks as defaults. The maximum number of
stacks is 64 with a size of 512 characters.

Generally, you should modify the default number of
stacks if requested to do so by LAN hardware or by one
of your application programs, or if you receive the error
message `Fatal: Internal stack failure,
system halted`.

The syntax for STACKS is

STACKS=*x,y*

where *x* is the number of stacks to allocate and *y* is the size of each stack.

Suppose that you have the setting

STACKS=9,128

To increase stacks, first increase the number of stacks. An example follows:

STACKS=12,128

Next, you may need to increase the stack size:

STACKS=12,256

RAM Disks

The Purpose of a RAM Disk

A RAM disk (also called a virtual disk) is an artificial disk drive by which a section of system memory (RAM) is set aside to hold data, just as if it contained actual disk sectors. To DOS, a RAM disk is the same as any other drive.

In ATs and other 80286 and 80386 PCs with large amounts of RAM, RAM disks are convenient for setting up frequently used programs in memory as though they reside on a floppy drive or for placing temporary working files in fast-access RAM to speed up program processing.

Note: All data resident on the RAM disk is lost when the PC is turned off.

Installing a RAM Disk

To install a RAM disk, you should include the following statement in your CONFIG.SYS file:

DEVICE=*d:path***VDISK.SYS** *p1 p2 p3* /**E:***nnn*

In the preceding statement, *d:path*\\ is the location of VDISK.SYS, *p1* is the size of the RAM disk given in kilobytes, and *p2* is the number of bytes per sector. The values for *p2* are 128, 256, or 512, with 128 as the default.

Finally, *p3* is the number of directory entries ranging from 2 to 512 with the default of 64, and /E:*nnn* tells VDISK to be installed in Extended memory with *nnn* as the number of sectors to be transferred at a time.

The following statement creates a 1.6M RAM disk with standard DOS 512-byte sectors and 256 entries in the directory:

    DEVICE=VDISK.SYS 1600 512 256

Caching

What Is a Disk Cache?

A disk cache is similar to the BUFFERS command in that it sets aside part of memory to act as a buffer between the hard disk and RAM. A disk cache temporarily stores data for faster access. When DOS requests a read from the hard disk, the cache software checks the cache memory to see whether the data is there before attempting to retrieve the data from the hard disk.

Expanded Versus Extended Memory

Caches use one of two kinds of available memory: Expanded and Extended.

The microprocessor used in pre-AT computers is the 8088 (or 8086) chip. This microprocessor has the capacity to address 1M of RAM. Because users and their programs required more memory, expanded memory was developed. Expanded memory allows a computer to have several megabytes of memory. Because the microprocessor can address only 1M, however, it can only "see" a portion of expanded memory. The computer must switch between 4 segments of 64K.

With the development of the AT computer came the capacity to address more than 1M of RAM. However, because DOS was designed to have a 1M memory limit, the additional memory that the microprocessor can address is called extended memory. Unlike expanded memory, extended memory does not have to switch

between segments of memory. OS/2 can take full
advantage of extended memory, using up to 16M of
RAM, but DOS cannot. A DOS system using expanded
memory can look at only 640K at a time and then must
switch in 64K increments to take advantage of the rest of
available memory in RAM. DOS doesn't support access
to extended memory, except for the creation of a RAM
disk and disk cache. Programs and data on DOS systems
cannot take advantage of extended memory. Special
programs such as Windows 386, however, can use
extended memory as expanded memory, while still
taking advantage of the 80386 processor chip.

Assume, for example, that you must fly from New York
to Los Angeles. On Expanded Airlines, you will have to
stop every 64 miles to check a map to see where you are.
If you board the Extended Express, however, you will
leave New York and fly nonstop to Los Angeles. From
this analogy you may realize that expanded memory is a
bit slower to use than extended memory, because
expanded memory is used only a portion at a time.

Cache Guidelines

For cache memory to be effective, it should be more
than 256K, and the cache memory should not reduce
DOS active program memory from 640K. This means
that the cache memory should run in expanded or
extended memory.

Using extended memory rather than expanded memory
eliminates the swapping in the reserved memory area by
DOS when it moves data from the cache to the programs
in RAM. A good cache memory program and a generous
amount of memory provide the best hard disk
performance.

A good cache program also reduces physical wear and
tear on the hard disk by reducing the number of times
that DOS reads the directory and FAT from the disk. A
bad or malfunctioning cache program, however, can
corrupt files on your disk with no outward indication.
Selecting and thoroughly testing a cache can easily be a
time-consuming task.

A sample cache is the one available when you purchase
a COMPAQ computer. To use the cache, include the

following statement in CONFIG.SYS for a 512K cache
in extended memory:

DEVICE=C:\BIN\CACHE.EXE 512 ON /EXT

Using AUTOEXEC.BAT

Along with CONFIG.SYS, which you use to configure
DOS, you can use the batch file AUTOEXEC.BAT to
set up some system defaults for each time you boot your
computer. Batch files in general are examined later.

You may use AUTOEXEC.BAT to set up a PATH (also
discussed later). Or you may use the AUTOEXEC.BAT
file to run certain programs each time you start your
computer. Examples of such programs include those
that copy your directory and FAT.

You may create the AUTOEXEC.BAT file with a text
editor such as EDLIN that comes with DOS or by typing

COPY CON AUTOEXEC.BAT

as explained later in the section on batch files.

A sample AUTOEXEC.BAT file is

ECHO OFF
CLS
PATH C:\DOS;C:\WP;C:\QB;C:\;
SET LIB=C:\QB
PROMPT d_[$p]
FR C: /SAVE

This batch file shuts off the display to the screen and
then clears the screen. The search paths are C:\DOS,
C:\WP, C:\QB, and C:\. An environment variable is set,
and the prompt is set to display the date, current drive,
and path. FR is the program from Norton Utilities that
saves a copy of the directory and FAT in case the hard
disk accidentally gets formatted. For a more complete
discussion of batch file commands, see the section
"STREAMLINING WITH BATCH FILES."

Using FASTOPEN

FASTOPEN is a feature provided for hard disks with DOS Version 3.3 and later. FASTOPEN retains copies of the locations of directories and recently opened files in RAM. FASTOPEN reduces the amount of time required to find the data on the hard disk because as files are accessed, FASTOPEN first searches the memory buffer area for information on the file before going to the hard disk to retrieve the information. This process significantly speeds up file access.

The syntax for FASTOPEN is

FASTOPEN *d:=nnn*

where *d:* is the hard disk to buffer and *nnn* is the number of directory entries to buffer—a number from 10 to 999. The default is 34. The FASTOPEN command can be included in your AUTOEXEC.BAT file.

The next step in preparing your hard disk for operation requires a plan for organizing the data and programs to be placed on the disk.

ORGANIZING DIRECTORIES

Because hard disks have such large capacities, the data stored on the disks must be organized so that it can be accessed easily by both the computer and the user. DOS, OS/2, and other operating systems use tree-structured directories.

What Is a Directory?

A directory or subdirectory is a logical (conceptual, as opposed to physical) area on the disk in which you store programs and data. Each directory or subdirectory functions similar to a single floppy disk. DOS commands establish and remove the subdirectories as well as allow you to move from subdirectory to subdirectory.

A tree-structured directory looks something like a common business organization chart. The position of the president is similar to the root directory at the top, and the locations of the vice presidents are similar to the subdirectories spread out underneath. If this structure is turned upside down, it resembles a tree with branches spreading out from the root.

A sample hierarchical directory structure showing the root directory and the subdirectories for the C drive is shown in figure 7 on page 47.

Advantages of Subdirectories

You should not store all your programs in the root directory for two good reasons. The first is that the root directory's size is limited; it can hold only 512 files. Second, you are presently restricted to 11 characters for a file name: 8 for the root name and 3 for the extension; therefore, different software vendors may use the same names for their files. One common name is INSTALL.EXE. You can keep INSTALL.EXE programs separated by placing them in their own separate subdirectories.

In contrast to the root directory, a subdirectory can contain any number of files. Besides containing files, a subdirectory can contain other subdirectories. *Note:* The terms subdirectory and directory may be used interchangeably.

Creating and Removing Subdirectories

You create and remove subdirectories by using the MD (Make Directory) and RD (Remove Directory) commands. A directory can be removed only when it is not the current directory and when it contains no files.

To create a directory, type

MD *dirname*

The backslash stands for the root directory, and *dirname* is the name of the directory you want to create. To make a subdirectory within another subdirectory, type

MD *\dirname\newdir*

Dirname must be a subdirectory already present on your hard disk.

To remove that directory, type

RD *\dirname*

Before a directory can be removed, it must be empty of files and subdirectories. Suppose that you want to delete the directory \DATA, for example, and it contains files and a subdirectory named \LETTERS. You must issue the following commands to remove completely both the directory and its subdirectory:

```
DEL \DATA\LETTERS\*.*
RD \DATA\LETTERS
DEL \DATA\*.*
RD \DATA
```

Changing Directories

To move between subdirectories, use the CD (Change Directory) command. With this command, you can specify the exact subdirectory to be accessed, or you may employ a short form of the command. CD is a command you will use most often when working with tree-structured directories on your hard disk. The syntax of the CD command follows:

To change to an exact subdirectory, type

CD *\subdir*

To change to one level up in the directory structure, type

CD ..

To change at that level across to the specified subdirectory, type

CD *..\subdir*

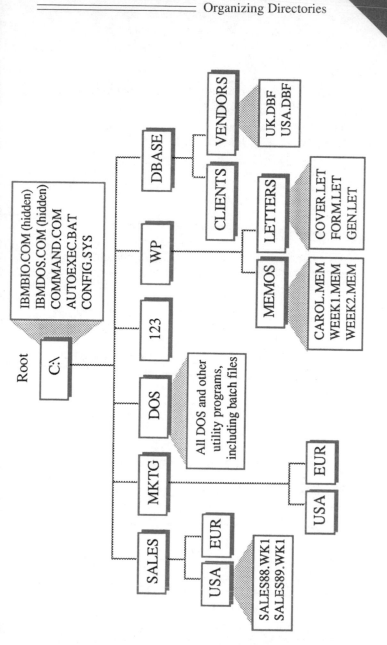

Fig. 7. Directory structure with multiple levels.

Uses of CD

Refer to the multilevel structure illustrated in figure 7 for the examples that follow.

To change from the root directory to the MKTG subdirectory, type the following:

CD \MKTG

You may move from one first level to another. If you are in the \MKTG directory and want to change to the \SALES directory, for example, type

CD \SALES

To move from the EUR to the USA subdirectory, you can use the long form of the CD command:

CD \SALES\USA

Or you can use the short form:

CD ..\USA

To move from USA or from EUR to SALES, you can use

CD ..

as well as

CD \SALES

To move from SALES to the root directory, you can use

CD ..

or

**CD **

Organization Strategies

How should you place the files on the disk to locate them easily, to upgrade DOS and applications software, and to access the data and program files rapidly from the hard disk? Following are some basic organizational hints to help you achieve these goals:

- Place as few files as possible in the root directory of your disk. The minimum files contained there should be IBMBIO.COM, IBMDOS.COM (both hidden), COMMAND.COM, CONFIG.SYS, and AUTOEXEC.BAT. All other files can be referenced when called from their subdirectories.

- Make the key files in the root directory Read-only (R) files by using the ATTRIB (Attribute) command so that they are not accidentally erased. To make all files in one directory read-only files, type

    ATTRIB +R *.*

- Keep separate directories for DOS, batch files (BAT), utility programs (UTIL), temporary work areas (TEMP), and project work areas (WORK1, WORK2).

- Make program subdirectory files Read-only (R) files, using the ATTRIB command.

- Keep the tree depth to as few levels as possible. Trees that are many levels deep may be more difficult to manage.

- Keep DOS paths short and tailored to the type of work you are performing (see the next section, "Understanding Paths"). If you have special programs with which you work, such as a scanner or desktop publishing program, set up the computer to use batch files to work specifically with that software. This approach will keep your search for files and data to a minimum. Once you shift to other, more standard programs, reset the DOS search paths to a normal operating format.

Understanding Paths

When your computer is booted, DOS usually sees the root directory first. You can use the PATH command to change the scope with which DOS looks for files.

When you are using DOS in a single subdirectory, DOS can see only the programs in that subdirectory. It does

not look at all the files on the disk. When DOS cannot
find something in the current directory, you can give it a
wider view of the disk by using the PATH command and
specifying that it look through several subdirectories.

What Are Paths?

You establish paths by using the PATH and APPEND
commands. These commands tell DOS where to search
for programs or data whenever the requested program or
data cannot be found in the current subdirectory. You
can display the current path for your system by typing

PATH

The syntax for establishing a path is

PATH *d:path1*\;*d:path2*\; ...

where *d:path1*\ is the entire first search path, *d:path2*\ is
the entire second search path, and ... is any other paths to
specify. You can use the semicolon to separate one path
from another.

The Rule of Defaults

The PATH command is limited to a total of 128
characters in DOS. PATH searches for files with COM,
EXE, and BAT extensions, and APPEND finds files
with any other extension. In the search process, DOS
first looks in the current directory. If the file specified is
not found there, DOS searches the first directory path
specified in the PATH statement, then the second path,
and so on, until the file is found. If the file is not found,
the message `Bad command or file name` is
displayed.

Absolute versus Relative Paths

PATH behaves strangely if the path is not specified
exactly. When you boot from your hard disk, you can set
the path to two directories by typing

PATH \DOS;\;

When you change from your hard disk to another
drive—to drive D, for example—DOS interprets the
path as for the new drive. Thus, DOS searches through
directories D:\DOS and D:\ for programs and not
through directories on drive C as intended. Specifying

the PATH directly and in full detail is best. In this case, the PATH statement should be

PATH C:\DOS;C:\;

Changing the System Prompt

While moving around on the hard disk, you can easily forget which directory is your current directory. You may change your system prompt to reflect the current directory by using the PROMPT command.

The syntax for the PROMPT command is

PROMPT *promptstring*

where *promptstring* is any text or metacharacter(s) or a combination of the two. Each metacharacter must be preceded by a dollar sign ($). A list of metacharacters follows:

PROMPT Metacharacters

Character	Use
Character	*Use*
$	$ (dollar sign)
_ (underscore)	Carriage return, line feed sequence
b	| (vertical bar)
d	Current date
e	Escape character (ASCII 1b hex, 27 decimal)
g	> (greater-than symbol)
h	Backspace character (ASCII 8, Ctrl-H)
l	< (less-than symbol)
n	Current drive letter
q	= (equal sign)
p	Current drive and directory
t	Current time
v	DOS version number

Here is an example of a PROMPT command:

PROMPT $d $t$hhh$_$p$g

The following prompt is produced:

```
                              Wed 3-08-1989 9:12:58
D:\TEMP >
```

The first line displays the date and time, and the second line identifies the drive and subdirectory to which you are pointing. The date and time are updated each time you issue a DOS command, which ensures that your system clock is set properly.

Note: The PROMPT command will not work properly unless ANSI.SYS is run each time your PC is started. Add the following line to your CONFIG.SYS to run ANSI.SYS:

DEVICE=C:\DOS\ANSI.SYS

To add this line, you must have a \DOS directory and the file ANSI.SYS in that directory.

Using APPEND

APPEND functions like the DOS PATH command but handles files not covered by PATH. PATH only searches for files with a BAT, COM, or EXE extension. APPEND tells DOS where to search for other data, such as auxiliary files for programs.

The syntax for APPEND is in two parts. The first part follows:

APPEND /E

The preceding part causes the next APPEND statement to attach to the environment with PATH:

APPEND=*d:path1*\;*d:path2*\;...

In the preceding statement, *d:path1*\ is the first APPEND path and *d:path2*\ is the second APPEND path.

To disconnect any assigned APPEND paths, type

APPEND;

To use APPEND most effectively, you should know
which programs need auxiliary files and specify only
those programs in your APPEND statement. When
WordPerfect starts, for example, it recalls where its
support files are stored by reading its configuration
information. Consequently, the APPEND command
does not benefit you here.

The path specified by the APPEND command may not
be the same path specified by the PATH command. For
example, even though your PATH statement is

PATH=C:\BIN;C:\WP;C:\PE;C:\DBASE4;C:\;

you may only set APPEND to be

APPEND=C:\BIN;C:\PE;

because these may be the only subdirectories that may
need to be searched for files not found in the path.

When programs are configured with the correct paths for
their support files, placing them in the APPEND-
specified path makes little sense.

Advanced DOS Commands

Some DOS commands can help with your hard disk
operation in special situations. These commands are
JOIN, SUBST, and ASSIGN.

JOIN

The DOS JOIN command combines a second disk to a
first disk's directory, making them a single disk. If you
have programs that need to use information from another
disk, you can use JOIN to make the two disks function
like a single disk. You can JOIN drive D to the
subdirectory C:\MKTG by typing

JOIN D: C:\MKTG

You can break the bonding of the drive to the
subdirectory by using

JOIN D: /D

SUBST

SUBST (Substitute) provides the mechanism for you to identify a subdirectory with a drive letter. Instead of referring to the data in C:\SALES\USA using the entire path specification, for example, you can refer to the data with a single drive G by typing

SUBST G: C:\SALES\USA

You can remove this substitution by entering

SUBST G: /D

The substitute drive letter must be within the LASTDRIVE= specification in the CONFIG.SYS file. If you specify drive G, for example, and your LASTDRIVE statement indicates only drives up to the letter F, SUBST returns an `invalid parameter` message.

ASSIGN

You can fool programs so that they think they're using one drive when they're actually using another. Suppose, for example, that an older program was written to store all its data on floppy drive B. You may want to store data on your hard disk, drive C. You can use the ASSIGN command so that when the program makes a request to drive B, it actually is making a request to drive C.

The syntax for ASSIGN is

ASSIGN *d1=d2* ...

where *d1* is the letter of the disk drive the program or DOS normally uses and *d2* is the letter of the disk drive you want the program or DOS to use. The ellipsis (...) signifies that you can make more than one assignment. If you want both drive A and drive B to refer to drive C, for example, enter the command

ASSIGN A=C B=C

MANAGING FILES

Setting up the hard disk properly and using fixed commands effectively are important. In addition, however, you must learn to organize and manage the files on your hard disk. Effective file management requires familiarity with some additional DOS commands and also requires a mechanism for naming shared data files—especially when your PC is connected to a LAN.

File-Naming Strategies

Guidelines for Naming Files

A file name is restricted to 11 characters: 8 characters for the root name and 3 characters for the extension. You also have restrictions on the names and characters that can be used. DOS device names such as CON, AUX, COM1, PRN, LPT1, and NUL cannot be used. Several characters are restricted from file names including the period (.), double quotes ("), slash and backslash (/,\), square brackets ([,]), vertical bar (|), greater-than and less-than symbols (>,<), plus sign (+), equal sign (=), semicolon (;), and comma (,).

Reserved File Names

Some file names have special meanings for DOS and therefore should not be assigned by the user. The two file names used by DOS to set up the operating environment of the computer are AUTOEXEC.BAT and CONFIG.SYS. Other names for files that you should not use include the types of files used by software manufacturers for installing their software. Some additional common names and extensions you may want to avoid are INSTALL, .BAK, .$$$, SETUP, START, HELP, SAMPLE, DEMO, TUTORIAL, and LEARN.

The goal in naming files is to permit management of file information by use of the name alone. Using like names can help you in grouping and managing files.

File Name Components

Careful specification of file names can give you powerful control over your data. The file name can be divided into three parts, reading left to right: the first four characters, the second four characters, and the extension.

```
FILE    NAME   .   EXT
1234    5678       123
```

You can use the first four characters to identify the project, customer, type of information, and so on. Use the second four characters to specify, for example, the date as either the month and year or the month and day. The extension is sometimes assigned by the program and sometimes specified by the creator. Lotus 1-2-3 assigns WK1 extensions to all its data files, for example, but WordPerfect allows you to define your own extensions.

Suppose that you have an account with Travelco, Inc., and are developing ads for the company's new winter travel brochure. You can name the file for this project TRBR8910.01. The first four characters identify the client (TR for Travelco, Inc.) and the product (BR for brochure). The last four characters identify the year and month of creation. The extension identifies the sequence in which the file was created. Notice that the year was placed before the month. When the data is sorted, the 1989 files will be together. When you reverse the year with the month, the files are grouped by month first and not by year.

Some sample file names from an archive directory follow:

```
SEMNAI86 ARC   287869   1-24-89  6:58p
SEMNDB86 ARC    49959   1-24-89  8:24p
SEMLIT88 ARC    36282   1-24-89  8:23p
SEMNLN88 ARC   686268   1-24-89  6:04p
SEMNPR89 ARC   252487   1-24-89  7:20p
```

The extensions for these files were assigned by an archiving program. File names were determined by the contents and the date. For example, SEMNLN88 is a file of notes for a seminar on understanding Local Area Networks produced in 1988, and similarly SEMNPR89 is an archive containing public relations documents, highlighting seminars produced in 1989.

The benefit of this approach to naming files is that by using the COPY command, you now can copy specific groups of files based on content and date into other subdirectories or onto floppy disks. Similarly, you can erase groups of files, change the attribute setting, and so on, using the file names just structured. Developing a logical structure to your filing system is a good idea, because the older a directory or file, the more difficult it becomes to identify the correct file to retrieve at any given time.

File Display Commands

Using Wildcards

The most often-used command for displaying the contents of your hard disk is DIR (Directory). This command lists the file name, extension, size of the file in characters, and date and time the file was created or last modified. By using DIR with the wildcard characters * and ? you can look at your hard disk directories and subdirectories in many ways. Suppose, for example, that you type the following:

DIR ????89*.*

The following files are scanned:

RPTH8903.01
UDCN8803.PAK
UTIL8901.PAK

And those files pertaining to 1989 are listed:

RPTH8903.01
UTIL8901.PAK

This sample display uses the file-naming structure and the DIR command described previously. The wildcard characters work with DOS and most other programs. In the following example, keep in mind that the file name is a maximum of eight characters and the extension is a maximum of three characters.

The wildcard characters function in

> **DIR ????89*.***

as follows:

- The * tells DOS to accept any character in this position and in any position to the right in the extension.

- The ? tells DOS to accept any character for these positions in the file name.

- Only the characters 8 and 9 are accepted in these positions by DOS.

Remember, the * matches any group of characters, and the ? matches any single character.

The DIR command can be used in a variety of ways. Following are some of the ways you can use DIR to produce a listing of your files:

DIR /W

Using this command creates a wide-screen display of the files in a directory showing only the file name and extension. The primary benefit here is that all files in a single directory appear on one screen.

DIR /P

This command creates a directory that displays the files 23 lines at a time. The 24th line displays the message `Strike a key when ready.` Pressing a key will display the next screenful of files. This command is handy when you need to find a single file in a directory that is too large to be displayed in its entirety on a single screen, and you need to display all the details—name, extension, size, and date/time—for the file.

---
*DIR *.*

This command gives you a quick way to display all the subdirectories in your current directory. It also displays all files with no extensions.

DIR *

With this command, you have a fast way to view the first-level subdirectories on a hard disk.

DIR>PRN

This command sends the directory listing to your printer, which is handy when you are planning hard disk organization. You also can combine this capability with some public domain programs to produce a printed copy of all the files on your hard disk.

DIR>filename.ext

This command causes the directory to be placed on the hard disk as a file—*filename.ext*. This command is complemented by

DIR>>*filename.ext*

which adds directory listings to the file *filename.ext*.

TREE and TREE /F

Use these commands to display the tree structure of your hard disk. These commands break down your directory system so that you can see all subdirectories and the files and subdirectories each directory owns.

Often, tree listings are very long, especially if you use TREE/F to display all files. You may want to type

TREE /F | MORE

This command lists a screenful of directory structure information, and then waits for you to press a key to display the next screenful.

CHKDSK /V

This command provides a similar display that is more condensed and may be more useful than the display produced by TREE /F, because the drive and path name are included in front of each file name.

Viewing the Contents of the Entire Hard Disk

Similarly, you can use CHKDSK to view the contents of
the entire hard disk by typing

CHKDSK /V | MORE

These commands provide you with timesaving methods
to view the disk contents or to copy entire areas of the
disk to another drive.

TYPE

The TYPE command displays a file's contents on the
screen. This DOS command must always be used with
the full file name (no wildcards). For example, you can
display the contents of your AUTOEXEC.BAT file by
entering

TYPE C:\AUTOEXEC.BAT

In this case, you see the text characters contained in the
AUTOEXEC.BAT file. If, in contrast, you use TYPE to
display the contents of FORMAT.COM or
COMMAND.COM files, you will be able to decipher
very little, because these files contain program codes for
the processor chip in your PC.

These are the basic file display commands used on the
hard disk. Following are more sophisticated ways that
DOS can work with hard disk files.

Selective File Listings

You can use several DOS commands—CHKDSK /V,
DIR, ATTRIB, FIND, SORT, and MORE—to produce
special displays of the files on your hard disk.

MORE

A program that manipulates the stream of standard-input
characters, one character after another, as they go to the
standard output is called a filter. The filter MORE sends
the file to the display 23 lines (one screenful) at a time.
MORE is helpful when you need to view all the files on
your hard disk. The prompt — More — is displayed at

the bottom of each screen when it is filled. Press a key to see the next screenful.

FIND

FIND selectively displays the lines that contain characters specified in quotes. The CHKDSK /V command can be even more selective when you use the FIND filter. You can display all files on your hard disk that have the extension COM by typing

CHKDSK /V | FIND ".COM" | MORE

This approach has limitations. The FIND filter only displays exact matches with the quoted characters. Because CHKDSK /V produces uppercase displays of the files on the disk, the characters in quotes must all be uppercase. For similar reasons, the wildcard characters will not work. Again, the exact match means that the ? or * must appear in the file name, which is not permitted by DOS.

Producing an Alphabetical Listing of Files

You can produce an alphabetical listing of the files and subdirectories of a single directory by typing

DIR | SORT | MORE

Viewing all Read-Only Files on Your Hard Disk

To view all read-only files on your hard disk, type

ATTRIB *.* /S | FIND " R "

Notice that there is one space on each side of the R. Without these spaces, every file with an R in it would be displayed.

You can produce the displays you want by using the DOS ATTRIB (Attribute) command. DOS ATTRIB displays and modifies file attributes. ATTRIB can work with the Read-only (R) and the Archive (A) attributes.

Sorting with a RAM Disk

If you have a RAM disk, you can speed up the sorting process noticeably by designating it as a default and performing the DIR command against the other drives. Suppose that you have RAM disk E and you want to

view a large sorted directory from drive C; type the
following at the E> prompt:

DIR C:*bigdir* | SORT | MORE

Copying Files

Duplicating files with the COPY and XCOPY
commands promotes file management and maintenance.
Often, when you change the contents of a file, you need
to keep a copy of the original. Or, in organizing your
disk, you copy software into specific directories.

XCOPY is designed primarily to work with hard disks
because its /S parameter permits you to copy files from
directories and subdirectories at the same time. COPY,
in contrast, is designed to work best with files on floppy
disks or files in a single directory and has no provisions
for working simultaneously with subdirectories. When
you are using COPY, the subdirectory must be specified
exactly.

The syntax of COPY is

COPY *ds:paths\\filename.ext dd:pathd*
  newname.ext

where *ds:paths\\filename.ext* is the drive, path, and file
name of the source file to be copied; and *dd:pathd*
newname.ext can consist of a drive name, drive name
and path, or drive name, path, and optional new file
name of the destination. If *newname.ext* is not given, the
file, when copied, has the same name as the source file.
Notice the following examples:

COPY C:\\DATA\\OLDFILE.TXT A:

**COPY C:\\DATA\\OLDFILE.TXT
  A:\\OLDFILE.BAK**

**COPY C:\\DATA\\OLDFILE.TXT
  A:\\NEWFILE.TXT**

The COPY and XCOPY commands use the wildcard
characters ? and * just as the DIR command does. Thus,

you can selectively copy files from one disk to another
or one subdirectory to another. COPY has several
parameters that are discussed next.

COPY /V

This option verifies that the sectors have been written to
the hard or floppy disk. Using this option is the same as
setting VERIFY ON in the AUTOEXEC.BAT file.
Setting VERIFY ON causes DOS to take extra time to
copy files. The benefit of VERIFY is that you have
greater assurance that the files can be read by DOS once
written. Typing

COPY C:\WPMEMO*.TXT A: /V

copies all files with the extension TXT from the
\WPMEMO subdirectory to the disk in drive A and
verifies the copy.

COPY /A

COPY /A treats the file as an ASCII (text) file. For
source files, DOS copies all information up to, but not
including, the first Ctrl-Z. For a destination file, DOS
adds a Ctrl-Z to the end of the file. This method of
copying files ensures that a good End-Of-File (EOF)
marker is placed in the file.

The following example uses the /A option looking for
the EOF character in each file as DOS combines (or
concatenates) A.BAT and B.BAT into the new file
C.BAT:

COPY /A C:\A.BAT+B.BAT B:\C.BAT

COPY /B

COPY /B treats the file as a binary (program) file.
Instead of depending on the End-Of-File marker, the file
size depends on the size given in the directory.

The /B option is the default used if no switch is given.
So the only time you will use the /B switch is if you use
/A in a COPY command and then want a file to be
treated as binary rather than ASCII. Here is an example:

COPY /A C.BAT /B D.BAT

XCOPY

XCOPY copies the files from directories and subdirectories at the same time, as opposed to COPY, which only deals with one directory at a time.

XCOPY has more options than COPY. The options are normally placed at the end of the command. XCOPY's syntax is basically the same as COPY 's syntax:

> **XCOPY** *ds:path\filename.ext dd:path\filename.ext*
> /**D:***date* /**M** /**A** /**S** /**E**

XCOPY is available with DOS 3.2 and later versions. The XCOPY options and their meanings follow:

XCOPY /A

This option causes XCOPY to copy only the files having the archive bit set. During the copy process, the archive bit is not reset.

XCOPY /M

This option also causes XCOPY to copy only the files having the archive bit set. In this case, however, the archive bit is reset during the copy process. When you use the ATTRIB command to display those files with the archive bit set, as described earlier, you can determine the files that will be backed up by XCOPY.

XCOPY /D:mm-dd-yy

This option causes XCOPY to copy files with the same date or a more recent date. Unfortunately, this option loses some of its potential because it cannot specify a range of dates such as 1-01-89 to 3-04-89.

XCOPY /S

This option has XCOPY search subdirectories as it copies. If a source directory from which to copy is specified, the /S option will only search subdirectories of the directory specified.

XCOPY /E

The /E option makes XCOPY create empty subdirectories on the target drive if the source drive has those subdirectories. The subdirectories are created regardless of whether those source drive subdirectories contain files. Normally XCOPY does not create subdirectories on the target drive if the source subdirectories do contain files.

Other XCOPY Options

/V causes XCOPY to verify that the data is properly written to disk. /P prompts you to confirm that you want the file copied. /W makes XCOPY wait for you to insert disks. If any problems are encountered with any files during the copy process, XCOPY halts and displays error messages. One message, Access denied, occurs if the target drive contains the same file that has the Read-only (R) attribute set. This message informs you that the copy process was not completed; you need to correct the problem and run XCOPY again.

Copying Files within the Same Subdirectory

To copy files in the same subdirectory with both COPY and XCOPY, you must rename the files during the copy process. If the files are not renamed, you may receive the Access denied or the File cannot be copied onto itself error message. To rename files during the copy process, type the following:

COPY *file1 newfile1*

This command creates a new file called NEWFILE1 in your directory or subdirectory. XCOPY produces slightly different results. When you type

XCOPY *file1 newfile1*

DOS responds with

```
Does NEWFILE1 specify a file name
or directory name on the target (F
= file, D = directory)?
```

You must respond by pressing **F**. DOS then completes
the copy and displays the following:

```
Reading source file(s)...
1 File(s) copied
```

Copying Files from One Subdirectory to Another

Copying between subdirectories using the COPY
command requires that you specify directories and
subdirectories. XCOPY is easier because you may use
the /S option. For an example, you can use the directory
structure shown in figure 7 on page 47. You can copy
the files from C:\SALES to C:\MKTG by using COPY
or XCOPY, but XCOPY makes the process quicker.

Using COPY, you need to type

COPY C:\SALES C:\MKTG
COPY C:\SALES\USA C:\MKTG\USA
COPY C:\SALES\EUR C:\MKTG\EUR

The result is that all files are copied from each directory
to its respective directory.

With XCOPY, the result is the same, but the command
is simpler. Type the following:

XCOPY C:\SALES C:\MKTG /S

XCOPY proceeds to copy all the files in the \SALES,
\SALES\USA, and \SALES\EUR subdirectories into the
\MKTG, \MKTG\USA, and \MKTG\EUR
subdirectories. The subdirectory structure is also
preserved.

With XCOPY, if the USA and EUR subdirectories do
not exist under \MKTG, those subdirectories will be
created and then the files will be copied to them. The
COPY command cannot create the nonexistent
subdirectories.

Copying All Files and Subdirectories within a Subdirectory

Using the example presented in the preceding section, to
copy all files from the directory SALES and the
subdirectories USA and EUR to a disk in drive B, you
can type the following:

XCOPY \SALES*.* B: /S /E

In this case, the contents of the directory and subdirectories, as well as their structures (the purpose of the /S switch), are copied in their entirety from the hard disk to the disk in drive B. The /E switch ensures that the empty directories will be created on drive B to maintain the structure.

Copying Files To Your Hard Disk

Which is the easiest way to move files from the hard disk to floppies and vice-versa? If you do not plan to copy simultaneously several subdirectories of files, COPY is just as easy to use as XCOPY. When you're copying large amounts of data, however, XCOPY takes less time than COPY. With just a few files, you may not receive any time savings, but when you are copying many files, XCOPY offers tremendous time savings. When you're copying 1,000K of files, XCOPY takes half the time as COPY. If you must copy from several subdirectories, XCOPY is the preferable command to use.

To copy files from drive A to your hard disk, follow these steps:

1. Use MD to create the subdirectory where you are going to place the files. For example, type

   MD \NEWDIR

2. Change to that subdirectory by using CD. For example, type

   CD \NEWDIR

3. Copy the files from the floppy by using

   COPY A:*.*.

Renaming Files

REN (Rename) is another handy DOS command for file management. REN can be especially convenient when used with read-only files.

The syntax for renaming a file is as follows:

   REN *oldname.ext newname.ext*

Here is an example:

REN SALES88.RPT NEWSALES.88

Rename can function even though the read-only attribute
of a file is on.

Removing Files

The commands for removing files from your drive are
DEL (Delete) and ERASE. Both commands yield the
same results. DEL is shorter and easier to type, so most
PC users prefer using it instead of ERASE.

The syntax to erase files is as follows:

DEL *filename.ext*

or

ERASE *filename.ext*

The key to using DEL or ERASE effectively is to be
careful with wildcard characters and the subdirectory to
which you are pointing.

If you choose to delete all files in a directory, you will
be prompted with the `Are you sure (Y/N)?`
message. You must answer **Y** and press Enter to erase
the files.

If you find that you are in the habit of eagerly pressing **Y**
at the `Are you sure (Y/N)?` prompt without first
verifying what you want to delete, you may want to
mark all your critical files as read-only so that even
when you type **DEL** *.* and press **Y**, the files are not
erased.

Deleting a File

Here is the preferred procedure for using ERASE or
DEL:

1. Change to the appropriate subdirectory by using CD.
   For example, type

   CD \SALES

2. Perform a DIR with the appropriate wildcard characters to ensure that the files you want to erase will indeed be erased. For example, type

DIR *.88

or

DIR SALES??.*

3. Issue the ERASE or DEL command. For example, type

DEL *.88

or

ERASE SALES??.*

In the following example, DEL may be easier. After you type

DIR SALES??.*

and verify that all files shown should be deleted, type

DEL

and then press the function key F3. The rest of the command is repeated so that you see the following on-screen:

```
DEL SALES??.*
```

Setting File Attributes

As described earlier, you can use ATTRIB to identify files that are marked with the Archive (A) and Read-only (R) attributes. ATTRIB also allows you to reset those attributes. Unfortunately, however, ATTRIB does not permit you to display and set the other file attributes.

Using ATTRIB and XCOPY, you can perform backups of your data to floppy disks without using the DOS BACKUP and RESTORE commands. Although BACKUP and RESTORE are designed specifically to perform the backup function, they also have an unpleasant pitfall. BACKUP and RESTORE come as a

matched pair. In other words, files that are processed
with BACKUP cannot be used unless you use
RESTORE.

ATTRIB and XCOPY are often preferable to the
BACKUP and RESTORE commands. ATTRIB and
XCOPY produce plain DOS file copies of those files
with the archive attribute set on your backup disk
instead of files that must be translated back to the hard
disk with RESTORE.

The syntax for using ATTRIB is

ATTRIB +R/-R +A/-A *filename.ext*

where + sets the attribute and - shuts off the attribute.
The R is for Read-only, and the A stands for Archive.

Checking File Attribute Settings

You can first check the archive attribute by typing

ATTRIB *.*

or

ATTRIB *.* | FIND " A "

Note: You must include the space on each side of the A.

Setting the Archive Attribute

When specific groups of files need to be backed up, you
can set the archive attribute by using

ATTRIB +A *filename.ext*

Once the archive attribute is set, you can use

XCOPY *filename.ext* **d**: **/M**

This command makes your backup copies and turns off
the archive bit.

Redirecting Input and Output

Redirection refers to changing the standard for input and
output. Normally, data is input from the keyboard and
output on the screen. In fact, the DOS devices STDIN

and STDOUT (standard input and standard output) are set to the keyboard and video display, respectively.

Using the < character tells DOS that the input should be received from the device or file on the right side of the < and sent to the program on the left side of the file. Using this character in a command is redirection of input.

The > character is used for redirection of output. The program on the left side of the > will be sent to the file or device on the right side of the > rather than the video display. Using two output redirection characters together causes the output to be appended—added to the file.

Piping is somewhat different. When you issue the pipe character, |, the result from the program on the left side of the | will become the input to the program on the right side of the |. You can think of this process as an actual pipe connecting the two programs.

You often will use > and < characters with the CHKDSK /V, ATTRIB *.*, and DIR commands to produce file outputs that can be used to create batch files. You can use the batch files to perform updates on many files at a single time on the hard disk.

The pipe character, |, is most often used with MORE, SORT, and FIND.

Creating a File by Redirecting the Output

You can create a file of all the files in their subdirectories by using

    CHKDSK C: /V>DISKCONT.ENT

If you need to add the files on drive D to the file, you can use

    CHKDSK D: /V>>DISKCONT.ENT

In this manner, the output from the CHKDSK on drive D is added to the original output from the CHKDSK performed on drive C.

Printing File Contents in DOS

To get a printout of file contents, type

    TYPE MYDOC.ASC>PRN

Redirecting Input

If you have a text file such as a large batch file called LONGFILE.BAT that cannot be displayed in its entirety with TYPE, you may use input redirection with MORE:

MORE<LONGFILE.BAT

MORE fills the screen and then waits for you to press a key before displaying the next screenful. MORE is useful in displaying long files. In this case, MORE gets its input from LONGFILE.BAT.

If you use

TYPE *filename.ext*

the file *filename.ext* is displayed on the screen. If this is a long file, most of the characters scroll off the screen. Piping the output of the TYPE command to MORE is convenient.

For example, the command

TYPE *filename.ext* **| MORE**

causes the *filename.ext* output to be given to MORE. MORE then displays *filename.ext* on the screen.

DISK OPERATIONS

Normally you boot your computer from your hard disk every day thinking nothing of it until something goes awry. Then panic may set in because all your data seems to be lost. Learning about disk operations can help resolve many hard disk problems.

Booting Your Hard Disk

Booting your hard disk requires performing one of the following:

- Turning the power switch on, if the machine is off
- Pressing Ctrl-Alt-Del

- Turning the power off and then on again (especially useful if the system is on but "locked up")

If your system is working properly, upon booting you will see the C> prompt (or whatever prompt you specified in your AUTOEXEC.BAT file). If a nonbootable floppy disk is in drive A, you will get an error message. If a bootable floppy is in drive A, you will see the A> prompt.

What Occurs in the Boot-Up Process

The sequence of events the system performs in the boot-up process follows:

1. The POST (power-on self test) diagnostics are performed, verifying that no serious hardware problems exist.

2. The partition table from the hard disk is read. This table is placed there by FDISK.

3. The master boot record is read from the hard disk. This record is placed on the hard disk when the DOS FORMAT command creates the directory and the FAT.

4. The root directory is read to search for the DOS program IBMBIO.COM. The FAT is read to search for the clusters comprising that program.

5. IBMBIO.COM is loaded into RAM.

6. IBMDOS.COM is loaded into RAM.

7. The programs specified in CONFIG.SYS are loaded in the sequence specified in the file; those at the top of the file are loaded first, and those at the bottom are loaded last.

8. COMMAND.COM is loaded from the disk to provide the C> prompt.

9. DOS performs the batch commands specified in the AUTOEXEC.BAT file.

Creating a Bootable Floppy Disk

In the event of problems, you can use a bootable floppy disk tailored to the exact configuration of your system. You can create this bootable floppy by formatting a floppy disk with the /S option and then copying your AUTOEXEC.BAT and CONFIG.SYS files to it. For example, type

FORMAT A: /S

A more thorough approach is to copy the programs specified in the AUTOEXEC.BAT and CONFIG.SYS files to the floppy as well as AUTOEXEC.BAT and CONFIG.SYS. Following is a typical AUTOEXEC.BAT file:

```
ECHO OFF
CLS
PATH C:\DOS;C:\WP;C:\;
APPEND /E
APPEND C:\DOS;
C\PCTOOLS\MIRROR C:;D
PROMPT [$P] $
```

To accompany the preceding batch file, you must also copy the programs APPEND and MIRROR onto the floppy disk. These programs need to be copied from their appropriate subdirectories onto the floppy. You may want to make an alternate modified AUTOEXEC.BAT file, naming it AUTOEXEC (no extension), that references only the floppy root directory as shown in this example:

```
ECHO OFF
CLS
PATH C:\DOS;C:\WP;C:\;
APPEND /E
APPEND C:\DOS;
MIRROR C:;D:
PROMPT [$P] $
```

Make the same types of changes to your CONFIG.SYS file on the floppy disk so that CONFIG.SYS works with programs on your hard disk and CONFIG works with the programs copied to your floppy disk. Other programs that should be copied to this disk are SYS.COM, FORMAT.COM, EDLIN.COM, FDISK.COM, BACKUP.COM, RESTORE.COM, and XCOPY.EXE.

If for any reason you cannot boot from your hard disk, you now can use this floppy to boot your PC. On the first try, use the copies of the AUTOEXEC.BAT and

CONFIG.SYS files that came directly from the hard disk. If these files work, the problem is probably that IBMBIO.COM, IBMDOS.COM, COMMAND.COM, AUTOEXEC.BAT, and/or CONFIG.SYS have been lost from the hard disk root directory. When the files are replaced, the system should boot properly. To replace the files, type

```
SYS C:
COPY COMAND.COM C:\
COPY AUTOEXEC.BAT C:\
COPY CONFIG.SYS C:\
```

When the original AUTOEXEC.BAT and CONFIG.SYS files don't allow you to boot the hard disk, make your alternate AUTOEXEC and CONFIG files into the AUTOEXEC.BAT and CONFIG.SYS files by renaming both sets of files, and retry the boot process. Once your system is booted, try to perform a DIR on the hard disk to see whether the drive is readable. If it is readable, the problem most likely is in the files referenced by the AUTOEXEC.BAT and CONFIG.SYS files. You can replace those files with fresh copies and retry the boot procedure from the hard disk alone.

Transferring the System

You can use the SYS command to transfer a copy of your operating system from a floppy disk to your hard disk. Issue the command executed from a bootable floppy by typing

```
SYS C:
```

The trick with the SYS command is that it transfers only the hidden IBMBIO.COM and IBMDOS.COM programs to the hard disk. Once the PC returns the system-transferred message, you must copy COMMAND.COM to the root directory of the hard disk.

Naming a Volume

DOS allows you to give your hard disk a name by using the LABEL command. Generally, floppy disks are not electronically labeled because most users put paper labels on the outside. Hard disks are different. When you are using more than one partition or more than a single drive, labeling each partition electronically with a different name is a good idea. The electronic label is displayed when you use the DIR command, so you can see with which partition or physical drive you are working.

The syntax for LABEL is

   LABEL *d:labelname*

where *d:* is the drive you want to label and *labelname* is a name of up to 11 characters. If *d:* is not given, the current drive is used, and if *labelname* is not given, you are prompted to type a label.

STREAMLINING WITH BATCH FILES

A batch file is simply a text file of DOS commands, one command per line, just as if typed from a DOS prompt. Batch files enable you to run a sequence of DOS commands by simply entering a minimum of one character.

Instead of always having to enter a particular sequence of DOS commands to run Lotus 1-2-3, for example, you can create a batch file to record your steps and shorten the process to the point where you just need to enter 123.

The original sequence follows:

   C: <Enter>
   CD \123 <Enter>
   123 <Enter>

By creating a 123.BAT file, you can replace that sequence with the following:

   123 <Enter>

Batch files reduce the amount of information you need to type when entering DOS commands. These files store the commands in text files that end with the extension

BAT. Batch files are easy to create, modify, and maintain with a text editor such as EDLIN. Because you are likely to create many batch files, placing them in a single subdirectory is a good idea. You may want to keep your batch files with your DOS and other utilities in a directory called \DOS. In this section, you will create some simple batch files and examine how they work.

Creating Batch Files

COPY CON

When creating a text file, such as a batch file, you do not necessarily need to have access to a text editor such as EDLIN. You may use the COPY command. Instead of copying from a disk drive, you copy from the console (CON), which is the keyboard. To create a batch file without a text editor, type

COPY CON *filename.ext*

where *filename.ext* is the name of the file to create. To create a file called MENU.BAT, for example, type

COPY CON MENU.BAT

and press Enter. When you press Enter, the cursor simply moves to the next line and waits for you to type something. Begin entering information, pressing Enter after each line. When you are finished, press F6, which produces a ^Z, or press the Ctrl-Z key combination. The ^Z character signals the end of the file. When you press Enter, the file is written to the disk. At that point, you can enter **MENU**, and the commands contained in the file MENU.BAT are processed.

The drawback to using COPY CON is that you can only edit the current line. Once you press Enter, you cannot make any further changes to that line. The only way to change what you have typed is to re-create the file and save it, or use EDLIN (or another text editor) to edit the file.

Batch File Commands

Many DOS commands are available for you to work
with in creating your batch files. In this section you will
see how they are to be used.

REM and PAUSE

You use the REM (Remark) command to place
comments in a batch file. At one time, REM was used to
display messages on the screen as a batch file was
running, but that purpose for the command was outdated
when ECHO was developed. (ECHO is discussed later.)

The REM statement is useful for placing documentation
in a batch file. After a few lines in a batch file, for
example, you may want to place a few REM statements
to explain what those lines accomplished. As the batch
file runs, the REM statement does absolutely nothing. Its
whole purpose is to provide internal messages to the
person editing the file.

The syntax for REM is

REM *remark to be made*

The PAUSE command stops batch file processing and
displays the message Strike a key when
ready, giving the user time to insert a disk into drive
A. When the user presses a key, the batch file continues,
copying the file.

The following batch file is an example of REM and
PAUSE:

```
@ECHO OFF
CLS
ECHO Insert a disk into drive A and
PAUSE
REM The above lines shut off the screen
REM display, clear the screen, and
REM prompt the user to
REM place a disk into drive A.
REM The PAUSE advises
REM the user to press a key to continue.
COPY C:\DATA\*.TXT A:
REM This line copies all text files
REM from \DATA to drive A.
```

ECHO

The ECHO command can prevent or allow screen display. Normally, batch files display each command as it is performed, which makes for cluttered displays. Using ECHO OFF stops the commands from being displayed. Once the ECHO OFF command is given, messages are displayed.

The syntax for ECHO is

ECHO ON/OFF

or

ECHO *message to echo*

For an example of both uses, create a file called MOVE.BAT by typing

```
ECHO OFF
DIR %1 | MORE
ECHO These files are about to
ECHO be moved to %2.
ECHO If any errors exist,
ECHO press Ctrl-Break now!
PAUSE
COPY %1 %2 /V
ERASE %1
```

Now follow the screen display after the command **MOVE STD*.* E:** is entered:

```
D:\ >MOVE STD*.* E:\

D:\ >ECHO OFF

Volume in drive D has no label
Directory of  D:\TEMP

STDPATHBAT 6   3-08-89   8:29a
STDPMPTBAT 8   3-08-89   8:30a
      2 File(s) 4796416 bytes free

These files are about to
be moved to E:\
If any errors exist,
press Ctrl-Break now!
Strike a key when ready . . .
STDPATH.BAT
```

```
STDPMPT.BAT
        2 File(s) copied
D:\ >
```

Notice that when you run the batch file, you see the
command `ECHO OFF`. After that, however, you do not
see any batch file commands. You only see the effect of
the commands. Also notice the effects of the two ECHO
message commands. Notice how the PAUSE command
sends the message `Strike a key when ready`
to the screen.

ECHO ON and the @ Symbol

You can modify the MOVE command by adding the @
symbol in the first line:

> **@ECHO OFF**
> **DIR %1 | MORE**
> **ECHO These files are about to**
> **ECHO be moved to %2**
> **ECHO If any errors exist,**
> **ECHO press Ctrl-Break now!**
> **PAUSE**
> **COPY %1 %2 /V**
> **ERASE %1**

As a result, the MOVE.BAT file runs exactly as in the
previous example, but the message `ECHO OFF` will
not be seen.

CLS

The CLS (Clear Screen) command clears the screen and
places the cursor in the upper left corner of the monitor.
In addition to batch files, CLS may also be entered at the
DOS prompt.

The syntax for CLS is

> **CLS**

Using CLS in a batch file clears the screen to get the
user's attention with new messages. Notice how the
MOVE.BAT file operates with the addition of the CLS
command:

> **@ECHO OFF**
> **CLS**
> **DIR %1 | MORE**

```
ECHO These files are about to
ECHO be moved to %2
ECHO If any errors exist,
ECHO press Ctrl-Break now!
PAUSE
COPY %1 %2 /V
ERASE %1
```

Now the MOVE.BAT batch command starts its display at the upper left corner of a cleared screen.

Batch File Parameters

In the batch file examples used so far, input has been received from the keyboard with the use of replaceable parameters specified as percent signs followed by numbers. MOVE.BAT uses %1 and %2, but you may use up to 10 parameters: %0 through %9. By typing in these replaceable parameters, you can enter specific parameters along with the batch command that the batch file may use.

A blank space separates the parameters on the command line—for example, MOVE STD*.* E:\. The replaceable parameter %0 represents the batch file name, MOVE. The parameter %1 becomes STD*.*, and %2 becomes E:\.

SHIFT

The batch file parameters can be specified in any batch command line. However, these parameters must be entered only at the time the batch file is invoked. You can use more than 10 replaceable batch file parameters by using the batch file SHIFT command. Create a batch file called PARAM.BAT:

```
:TOP
ECHO %0 %1 %2 %3 %4
SHIFT
IF NOT %0.==.GOTO TOP
```

Next execute PARAM.BAT, specifying the following:

```
PARAM A B C D
```

The results are shown in the following screen:

```
C:\ >PARAM A B C D

C:\ >echo PARAMABCD
PARAMABCD

C:\ >shift

C:\ >pause
Strike a key when ready . . .

C:\ >IF NOT A.==. GOTO TOP

C:\ >ECHO ABCDE
ABCDE

C:\ >shift

C:\ >pause
Strike a key when ready . . .

C:\ >IF NOT B.==. GOTO TOP

C:\ >ECHO BCDEF
BCDEF

C:\ >SHIFT

C:\ >PAUSE
Strike a key when ready . . .

C:\ >IF NOT C.==. GOTO TOP
 .
 .
```

Notice that each time SHIFT is used, what was assigned to %0 is gone. Then all the parameters specified on the command line shift down by one parameter. In this sample batch file, when all parameters have been used, the batch file will stop.

Other Batch File Commands

GOTO, IF, FOR..IN..DO, and CALL are powerful and advanced commands that give you fundamental programming capabilities in batch files. Because these commands are advanced, they aren't used as often as other commands. In this section, however, you will develop an understanding of how these commands work so that you can use them properly in your batch files.

GOTO

The syntax for GOTO is

GOTO *label*

Sometimes you will want to change the order of operation of a batch file. You can do so with GOTO. GOTO is always followed by a label. A label is an eight-character word preceded by a colon. When the GOTO command is given, the batch file is searched for the label. If the label is found, then execution of the batch file begins on the statement after the label. For example, look at this batch file:

```
:LABEL1
ECHO Hello
GOTO LABEL1
```

This batch file, when run, will continue forever or until Ctrl-Break is pressed. Notice the label :LABEL1. This line is just a marker and has no action in the batch file. The text Hello is echoed to the screen; then the GOTO LABEL1 causes the batch file to start over. GOTO isn't always used as a looping device, however. Sometimes GOTO is used to skip parts of a batch file, as demonstrated in "Sample Batch Files."

IF

IF allows for true/false testing in a batch file. Uses for this command include testing for the existence of a file, testing for equality of two items, or testing for an error:

```
IF EXIST filename.ext
IF string1==string2
IF ERRORLEVEL number
```

Generally, on the same line with the test, you will insert a command that will be executed if the test is true. For an example, create the following batch file called TESTIF.BAT:

```
IF %1.==HELLO. ECHO You typed HELLO
IF EXIST TESTIF.BAT ECHO Found
    TESTIF.BAT
FORMAT A:
```

> **IF ERRORLEVEL 1 ECHO Problem found during FORMAT**

To run the batch file, type (in uppercase)

> **TESTIF HELLO**

You will see that the first statement tests whether parameter 1 is HELLO. Because it is, the message `You typed HELLO` is echoed to the screen.

The next test is for the existence of the file TESTIF.BAT. Because this is the file you ran, it does exist. The statement is true, and the message `Found TESTIF.BAT` is echoed.

The third statement in the preceding batch file formats a disk in drive A. Make sure that no disk is in drive A and press a key to start formatting. When the error message is displayed and FORMAT wants to know whether you want to format another, press N and then press Enter. FORMAT passes a code back that an error occurred (the drive was not ready). The message `Problem found during FORMAT` appears.

Error codes are 0 for normal operation and then 1 through 255 for any abnormal operation—for errors. Testing for the ERRORLEVEL 1 will actually find any error code of 1 or greater. So if you are testing for several error codes, test for the highest error code number first.

FOR..IN..DO

You can use the FOR..IN..DO command to repeat a command. The syntax for FOR..IN..DO is

> **FOR %%d IN (set) DO command %%d**

where %%d is a variable, *set* is a string or strings to replace the variable, and *command* is a command to execute, normally with the variable.

Suppose, for example, that this command is in a batch file:

> **FOR %%f IN (*.BAT *.TXT) DO COPY %%f A:**

When the command in the batch file is executed, %%f becomes *.BAT. The command COPY *.BAT A: is activated. When all batch files have been copied, FOR..IN..DO moves to the next string in the set, which is *.TXT. Then *%%f* becomes *.TXT, and the command COPY *.TXT A: is activated. When all strings in the set have been exhausted, batch file execution continues with the next line.

CALL

CALL allows you to "nest" batch files. Suppose, for example, that you start a batch file. When the batch file encounters a CALL statement, the batch file will automatically run another batch file. When the second batch file is completed, execution returns to the first batch file at the line after the CALL.

The syntax for this command is

CALL *batchfile*

Try out CALL with the batch files BATCH1.BAT and BATCH2.BAT:

BATCH1.BAT

```
ECHO this is BATCH1
CALL BATCH2
ECHO have returned to BATCH1
```

BATCH2.BAT

```
ECHO have entered BATCH2
```

Start BATCH1. You will see the first message from BATCH1 and then the message from BATCH2. Finally, you will see the second message from BATCH1.

Consider using CALL in AUTOEXEC.BAT. Have AUTOEXEC.BAT call other batch files to set your prompt and path. If the prompt or path is altered as you are working in DOS, you don't need to rerun AUTOEXEC.BAT to reestablish your standard operating environment. First review how the STDPATH.BAT and STDPMPT.BAT files were created and combined into the AUTOEXEC.BAT file.

Here are the commands:

STDPATH.BAT

```
PATH C:\;C:\DOS;C:\UTIL;C:\DBASE;
   C:\123;C:\WP;
```

APPEND C:\;C:\DOS;C:\UTIL;
   C:\DBASE;C:\123;C:\WP;

STDPMPT.BAT

PROMPT $e[1A$e[52C$d thhh $p $g
VERIFY ON

AUTOEXEC.BAT

CALL STDPATH
CALL STDPMPT
FASTKB
FLASH 256 /M=ET

When the AUTOEXEC.BAT file is executed, the batch files STDPATH and STDPMPT are called; these files set the standard path and prompt. Next, FSTKB is executed. FSTKB is a program for speeding up movement of the screen cursor. Finally FLASH, a disk cache program, starts.

If you need to change the standard path or prompt, you can (see "Changing the System Prompt"). To set the path or prompt to standard, simply run STDPATH or STDPMPT rather than AUTOEXEC.BAT. If you run the AUTOEXEC.BAT again, the programs FASTKB and FLASH run again, which is unnecessary.

Sample Batch Files

Often, the easiest way to understand how commands work is to see them in action. This section lists a few useful batch files so you can examine further how batch commands work.

FORMAT.BAT

Many computers have one 5 1/4-inch drive and one 3 1/2-inch drive. Often, both are high-density drives but can format a double-density disk. To format a double-density disk on a high-density drive, you must remember many different options of FORMAT.

An alternative is to set up the batch file FORMAT.BAT, which does all the work for you. All you have to remember is that a 5 1/4-inch double-density disk is 360

(360K) and that a high-density disk is 12 (1.2M). A 3 1/2-inch double-density disk is 720 (720K), and a high-density disk is 144 (1.44M).

Note: This batch file will only allow you to format a floppy disk. No provision exists for formatting your hard disk.

To use the following FORMAT.BAT file on your system, you must first rename FORMAT.COM to XFORMAT.COM and make sure that the file is in a subdirectory called C:\DOS. Also make sure that the 5 1/4-inch drive is drive A and the 3 1/2-inch drive is drive B.

The syntax is

FORMAT *size option*

where *size* is 360, 720, 12, or 144 (as described previously) and *options* is either /S or /V to transfer the operating system or assign a volume label, respectively. Now enter the batch file FORMAT.BAT:

```
@ECHO OFF
CLS
REM Test for proper sizes
IF %1.==. GOTO EMPTY
FOR %%s IN (360 720 12 144) DO IF
%1.==%%s. GOTO F%%s
GOTO WRONGSIZE
REM Each label for disk size settings
:F360
SET DRIVE=A:
SET DENSITY=/N:9 /T:40
SET OPTIONS=%2
GOTO FMT :F720
SET DRIVE=B:
SET DENSITY=/N:9 /T:80
SET OPTIONS=%2
GOTO FMT
:F12
SET DRIVE=A:
SET DENSITY=
SET OPTIONS=%2
GOTO FMT
:F144
SET DRIVE=B:
SET DENSITY=
```

```
SET OPTIONS=%2
GOTO FMT
:FMT
ECHO Drive=%DRIVE% - Size=%1 -
Options=%OPTIONS%
C:\DOS\XFORMAT %DRIVE% %DENSITY%
%OPTIONS%
GOTO END
REM Displays HELP for syntax errors
:EMPTY
ECHO You did not enter a size.
ECHO .
GOTO HELP
:WRONGSIZE
ECHO You typed an incorrect size.
ECHO .
:HELP
ECHO Your command was %0 %1 %2 %3
ECHO .
ECHO The proper syntax is
ECHO .
ECHO .  FORMAT [size] [options]
ECHO .
ECHO where [size]=360, 720, 12, 144 and
ECHO [options] is /s or /v.
GOTO END
:END
FOR %%e IN (DRIVE DENSITY OPTIONS)
DO SET %%e=
```

MOVE.BAT

The batch file that follows is actually made up of three separate batch files. You can include labels in batch files to flag various locations to which batch files can branch. You also can achieve branching by creating separate batch file modules that support a central batch file, as in the following example.

The following batch file uses the CALL command. Remember that CALL allows a batch file to transfer control to another batch file, return to the originating batch file, and continue where it left off. The command also permits passing replaceable parameters to the called batch files, but new parameters cannot be returned. The batch file that follows uses the environmental variable DEXIST. The environment is a safe area of RAM established to hold information. An environmental variable provides a noninteractive method to give your programs information. When DIREXIST.BAT is called, it signals the main module (MOVE.BAT) through DEXIST. DEXIST tells MOVE.BAT whether a directory exists.

In this example, each module is listed with its respective name. You must always use the module's exact name; the batch file simply will not work if the same names are not used throughout the listing.

MOVE.BAT

```
@ECHO OFF
CLS
IF %2. == . ECHO %1 being copied to the
    current directory
IF %1. == . GOTO NOCOPY
CALL DIREXIST %2
IF %DEXIST%==FALSE GOTO NOCOPY
FOR %%a IN (%1) DO CALL MV %%a %2
GOTO END
:NOCOPY
ECHO Either you did not enter the source and
ECHO destination or the path %2 was not
    found.
ECHO .
ECHO The proper syntax is:
ECHO .
ECHO . MOVE source destination
ECHO .
:END
```

DIREXIST.BAT

```
@ECHO OFF
ECHO TEST > c:\XXX
IF EXIST %1 GOTO FILEHERE
COPY c:\XXX %1 > NUL
IF EXIST %1\XXX GOTO CLNUP
SET DEXIST=FALSE
GOTO END
:FILEHERE
SET DEXIST=FALSE
ECHO %1 is a file, not a directory
GOTO END
:CLNUP
```

```
SET DEXIST=TRUE
DEL %1\XXX
:END DEL c:\XXX
```

MV.BAT

```
@ECHO OFF
ECHO Moving %1 to %2
COPY %1 %2 /V > NUL
DEL %1

@ECHO OFF
ECHO TEST > c:\XXX

@ECHO OFF
ECHO Moving %1 to %2
COPY %1 %2 /V > NUL
DEL %1
```

Testing Batch Files

In testing a batch file, you may not always want to run the program the batch file was meant to run. For example, consider the FMT.BAT batch file that is used to prevent your hard disk from being formatted:

FMT.BAT

```
@ECHO OFF
CLS
IF %1.== C: GOTO END
FORMAT %1
:END
```

If the user types

    FMT C:

the IF test becomes true and the batch file ends, preventing the hard disk from being formatted. If the user types a lowercase c rather than an uppercase C, however, the IF test becomes false and the hard disk may be formatted.

While you are testing this batch file, you do not want to find that using a lowercase c can format your hard disk. Rather, use CALL and a second batch file. The second

batch file, called TESTBAT.BAT, may appear as
follows:

```
REM This is a test batch file
ECHO You have entered TESTBAT
ECHO with the parameter %1
```

Now, for testing purposes, replace the line FORMAT
%1 in the FMT.BAT file with the line TESTBAT %1.
When you run the FMT.BAT file, you will find that a
lowercase c causes TESTBAT.BAT to execute. By
following this procedure, you safely can find that you
need to do more work to the FMT.BAT file.

Batch File Strategies

Batch files are great for organizing your hard disk and
optimizing its use. Most of the time, you operate your
system by using specific programs such as a word
processor or a spreadsheet. Occasionally, you use other
programs such as a database package, a separate spelling
checker, or maybe a desktop publishing package with a
scanner.

Setting up your system to operate with any one of these
packages at any time can easily result in a cumbersome
path. You can organize PC operations much better with
a menu and batch files that configure your system
precisely for the type of work you are performing.

Setting Up Batch File Menus

When your PC boots, have the AUTOEXEC.BAT file
set up your system for normal or standard operation.
Then create two files called HELP.BAT and
HELP.TXT. The HELP.TXT file will contain your menu
display, and the HELP.BAT file will contain just the
instructions to display your HELP.TXT file.

Create HELP.BAT by using an editing program or by
typing

```
COPY CON C:\BAT\HELP.BAT
```

Then enter the following single line of instructions:

HELP.BAT

TYPE C:\DOS\HELP.TXT

Next create a help display similar to the one that follows by using an editing program (the easiest way) or using COPY CON C:\BAT\HELP.TXT:

```
                    MAIN MENU

    Type the number preceding the entry
    to run the software identified:
       1. Ventura
       2. WordPerfect
       3. Procomm
       4. Personal Editor
       5. Lotus 1-2-3
       6. dBASE
       7. Park Disk Heads
       8. Other programs
```

After you complete the help display, you need to create batch files 1.BAT, 2.BAT, 3.BAT, 4.BAT, 5.BAT, 6.BAT, 7.BAT, and 8.BAT. These files will set up your system for operation with that specific software. To run WordPerfect, for example, you need to create the batch file 2.BAT as follows:

2.BAT

@ECHO OFF
CLS
C:
CD \DATA\LETTERS
WP
**CD **
HELP

When you press 2 and then press Enter, the batch file first shuts off the echo and clears the menu from the screen. Next, C: ensures that you are on drive C, in case you had been using a different drive. The directory is changed to a common directory called \DATA\LETTERS, which contains letters created with WordPerfect. WP starts WordPerfect. This batch file assumes that your PATH was set in your

AUTOEXEC.BAT file and that the WordPerfect subdirectory is on that search path.

When you exit WordPerfect, control returns to the batch file. The root directory becomes the current directory, and the HELP batch file is run again to return the menu to the screen. Each of the numbered batch files should resemble 2.BAT. The final statement should start HELP to bring back the MAIN MENU when programs are exited.

With the HELP.BAT file, if you cannot remember which menu entries are available, you may type **HELP** anywhere to display the HELP.TXT message. The \DOS directory is always in your path, and the HELP.BAT file tells TYPE exactly where the HELP.TXT message resides on your hard disk.

Special Batch Files

To find files with specific extensions or names, or in specific subdirectories, enter

FFILE.BAT

```
@ECHO OFF
CLS
CHKDSK /V | FIND "%1" | MORE
```

To show all files and subdirectories on the hard disk sorted in alphabetical order, enter

SFILE.BAT

```
@ECHO OFF
CLS
CHKDSK /V | SORT | MORE
```

To display sorted files in a directory, enter

SDIR.BAT

```
@ECHO OFF
CLS
DIR %1 | SORT | MORE
```

To find files with specific attributes and to sort them in alphabetical order, enter

FSFILE.BAT

```
@ECHO OFF
CLS
CHKDSK /V | FIND "%1" | SORT | MORE
```

To perform a find and sort from your RAM drive E, speeding up operation, enter

FSEFILE.BAT

```
@ECHO OFF
CLS
E:
CHKDSK /V | FIND "%1" | SORT | MORE
```

To find the files marked with the read-only attribute, enter

FRFILE.BAT

```
@ECHO OFF
CLS
ATTRIB *.* /S | FIND " R "
```

To find the files marked with the archive attribute, enter

FAFILE.BAT

```
@ECHO OFF
CLS
ATTRIB *.* /S | FIND " A "
```

To show all the read-only attribute files on a hard disk sorted in alphabetical order, enter

FSRFILE.BAT

```
@ECHO OFF
CLS
ATTRIB %1\*.* /S | FIND " R " | SORT
  | MORE
```

These batch files are based on DOS commands that were discussed previously. The batch files help you run those DOS commands because they reduce the amount of typing you must do and let you know where uppercase letters are needed in the command.

HARD DISK MAINTENANCE

By performing general maintenance, you can effectively reduce hard disk problems and prolong the life of your hard disk. Even with proper maintenance, however, all hard disks do have a limited life.

The Lifespan of a Hard Disk

Early disks were designed to operate for 10,000 power-on hours. That amount of time is equal to about 5 years of operation, 8 hours per day, 5 days per week, and 50 weeks per year. Today's hard disks will operate an average of 35,000 to 50,000 hours before failing.

Eventually, all hard disks fail. Because the directory and FAT are used most often, they are likely to be the first areas to lose data. When the directory and FAT lose data, the disk is unusable. Some hard disk preparation programs, such as On-Track System's Disk Manager program, allow you to move the directory and FAT to cylinders other than the beginning cylinders on the disk, therefore extending the life of some disks.

Of course, ultimate protection comes from periodic and regular backups, discussed later in this section.

Hard Disk Hazards

Awareness of the daily threats to your hard disk and proper care can prevent many different types of hard disk problems.

You can perform simple hard disk maintenance by doing the following:

- Park the heads when you're leaving the computer unattended or moving the computer.

• Keep the room temperature stable. If the temperature varies significantly, leave the computer on to
minimize its internal temperature fluctuations. If
you leave the computer on, connect it to a good
surge suppressor to prevent electrical damage from
power surges due to storms, etc.

Manufacturers' Design Defects

Any time you use a mechanical product, you can
have trouble with it. Be sure to buy from a reputable
dealer who will assist you in correcting problems.
For example, the original IBM PC AT hard disks
designed by CMI had defects. Two different models
of CMI drives had problems. Seagate once
manufactured a batch of ST-225 drives that failed
after about a year's operation.

Vibration Hazards

The greatest threat to the operation of hard disks is
vibration. Parking the hard disk heads when the
drive is powered off does not protect from head
crashes caused by vibration when the disk is
operating. Are your hard disk and printer on the
same table or stand? If so, you are risking problems
with your drive. The vibration from the printer can
cause the heads to crash. As the disk ages, the
printer's vibration becomes more of a threat to the
valuable data stored on the disk's surface.

Using a head parking program is helpful any time
you leave your computer while it is operating.
Public domain head parking programs include
TIMEPARK, a memory-resident program that parks
the heads automatically after 1 to 10 minutes, and
the DPARK programs. Mace Utilities also includes
a disk head-parking program.

Temperature Shock

Leaving your computer turned off overnight and on
weekends causes it to become chilled during the
winter months. When you restart the computer, the
internal temperature can climb from a starting point
of 40 to 60 degrees Fahrenheit to 80 to 100 degrees,
within the period of 20 minutes. The result is

internal stress on hard disk components that have tight tolerances (hard disk heads fly closer to the hard disk surface than half the diameter of a human hair). Severe strain can cause head crashes or difficulties. Leaving the computer turned on all the time helps alleviate the temperature shock problem, but it also can shorten the life of the drive. If you frequently use the computer, you may want to leave it on all the time; if you seldom use the computer and keep it in a temperature-stable environment, turn it off when you're not using it to make the drive last longer.

Portable and laptop computers with hard disks should always be kept reasonably warm. (A good rule is that if you are comfortable with the room temperature, it is the proper temperature for your computer system.) Never leave portable and laptop computers overnight in an automobile during times of excessive heat or cold.

Hard Disk Problems

Even if you take proper care of your hard disk, many hard disk problems are unavoidable. Hard disk problems can be grouped into three main classes:

Head Crashes

Head crashes destroy the hard disk surface and data in those areas on the surface. The most serious head crashes are those that destroy the master boot record, the FAT, or the directory. All data on the disk can be lost. However, many hard disk head crashes are recoverable. If a bad area occurs in the directory or the FAT because of a head crash and your PC displays the SECTOR NOT FOUND or FILE ALLOCATION TABLE BAD, DRIVE C ... ABORT, RETRY, FAIL message, you can generally recover data with the latest versions of Mace Utilities or Norton Utilities. Mace Utilities permits you to read your disk even when the boot sector has been corrupted. A special program bypasses the DOS error messages and permits you to copy the disk contents to a backup media.

Electronic Defects

You may have problems with your hard disk's controller electronics or the drive electronics. Semiconductor electronics rarely fail, but it is possible. You usually can fix a faulty controller board in a PC by replacing the defective board. In XTs, the controller board often becomes inseparable from the specific hard disk that is installed. Other controllers may not work with that hard disk unless a physical format is performed with that specific drive attached to that specific controller. Unfortunately, the physical format destroys all data on the disk.

Motor Problems

Motor problems cause the hard disk to cease rotation or stop head movement. Hard disk motor problems are not recoverable. If the disk does not rotate up to the proper operating speed, for example, it cannot be read. When the head positioning motor fails, again no recovery is possible. When the heads are not moved over the data, they cannot read the hard disk. Your only alternative in these cases is to send the hard disk to a repair service that specializes in recovering your data.

The recovery strategy for hard disk problems is to make DOS and your computer think that the disk is working properly by using one of the utilities mentioned. After you accomplish this task, you may be able to read the directory and FAT. If the FAT is defective, a second copy of the FAT may be used in recovering the files from the disk. *Note:* As soon as possible, copy the files from the hard disk to a backup media or drive.

Analyzing Your Hard Disk

CHKDSK, the most misunderstood of the DOS commands used with hard disks, is your first line of defense when correcting hard disk problems. Before you can understand CHKDSK, however, you need to examine the structure of the directory and File Allocation Table (FAT). A sample directory entry pointing to the FAT is shown in figure 8.

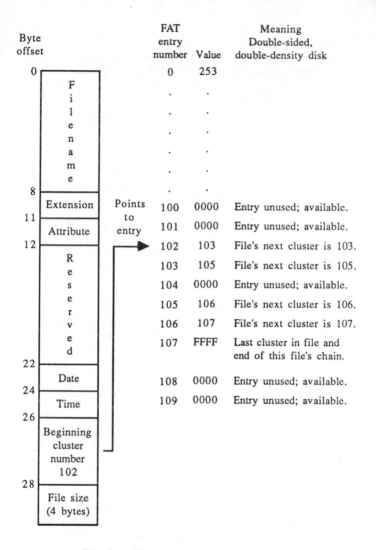

Fig. 8. A file made up of five clusters chained together.

Understanding Directory and FAT Entries

The directory entry contains the information you see
when using the DIR command. The entry contains the
file name, extension, size of the file in bytes, and date
and time the file was created or last modified. The
directory entry also contains one piece of information
that you do not see: the pointer to the first FAT table
entry. The pointer is a number. In this case, FAT entry
102 is the beginning cluster number for the file. You
may recall that a cluster is one or more sectors,
depending on the disk size. It is the basic unit in which
disk space is allocated.

When you move to cluster 102, you find that it contains
the value 103. Next in the chain of clusters making up
the file is cluster 103. Chains are a series of clusters that
contain the data in the file. Cluster 103 points to cluster
105. Clusters 102 and 103 make up one block of
contiguous clusters in the file. Cluster 105 points to
cluster 106, and cluster 106 points to 107. Cluster 107
contains all 1s (FFFF), signifying End-Of-File and thus
that this is the last cluster in the chain. Clusters 105,
106, and 107 make up the second and final block of
contiguous clusters in the file.

With an understanding of the relationship between the
directory and the FAT, you are now ready to learn how
CHKDSK works.

CHKDSK

The syntax for CHKDSK is

CHKDSK *filename.ext* /V /F

where *filename.ext* is a file or group of files on your hard
disk. This command determines whether individual files
are stored as a contiguous unit or scattered throughout
areas of your hard disk.

/V verifies and displays all files in all subdirectories, and
/F fixes errors in the directory and FAT.

CHKDSK *.* /V

Whenever you suspect problems with your hard disk,
you should issue the command **CHKDSK *.* /V**

Remember, however, that this command only corrects conflicts between the directory and the FAT. Following is a listing of nontypical (normally, you do not get so many errors) CHKDSK output for a floppy disk so that you may examine five fairly common error messages:

```
Directory C:\
   C:\ARC520.COM
   C:\BWVID.ARC
   C:\CDISK.ARC
   C:\CORETEST.ARC
C:\FASTCOPY.ARC
Errors found, F parameter not
specified. Corrections will not be
written to disk.

C:\FASTCOPY.ARC
   Allocation error, size adjusted.
C:\HDAT.ARC
C:\HDTABL.ARC
C:\MIPS.ARC

29 lost clusters found in 7 chains.
Convert lost chains to files
(Y/N)? n
29696 bytes disk space would be
freed.

A:\FASTCOPY.ARC
A:\HDAT.ARC
   Is cross linked on cluster 255
A:\MIPS.ARC
   Is cross linked on cluster 255
362496 bytes total disk space
319488 bytes in 25 user files
13312 bytes available on disk

720896 bytes total memory
165008 bytes free

A:\FASTCOPY.ARC
   Contains 2 non-contiguous blocks.
A:\HDAT.ARC
   Contains 2 non-contiguous blocks.
```

Interpreting CHKDSK Error Messages

The preceding CHKDSK procedure presents five error messages:

1. `Errors found, F parameter not specified. Corrections will not be written to disk.`

2. `Allocation error, size adjusted.`

3. `29 lost clusters found in 7 chains. Convert lost chains to files (Y/N)? n 29696 bytes disk space would be freed.`

4. `Is cross linked on cluster 255`

5. `Contains 2 non-contiguous blocks.`

An examination of these error messages follows:

The `Errors found, F parameter not specified. Corrections will not be written to disk` message signals that CHKDSK has encountered errors between the directory and the FAT. This message also states that none of the errors will be corrected at this point, which is precisely what you want if you are going to save any existing files off the disk. Once the /F parameter is specified, CHKDSK writes changes to the disk and some data may be overwritten.

The `Allocation error, size adjusted` message signals that the file identified above it has a file size not consistent with the number of clusters in the FAT, which usually means that the directory entry shows a 50K size and no clusters in the chain for the file. Thus, the FAT suggests that the file size is zero and that CHKDSK is going to adjust the file size to zero when the /F parameter is specified.

The `29 lost clusters found in 7 chains. Convert lost chains to files (Y/N)? 29696 bytes disk space would be freed` message indicates that some chains in the FAT have no attached file names. When CHKDSK converts the chains to files, you find in the root directory files with the names `FILE0000.CHK`, `FILE0001.CHK`, and so on.

Often, this is unassigned disk space from old files, and the files can be erased. However, use the TYPE command to check each file, starting with FILE0000.CHK. This file may contain data that you want to keep, perhaps from a file with an error. Copy the files to a floppy disk.

The message Is cross linked on cluster 255 signals that two or more files are pointing to the same cluster. Usually, when two or more files point to the same cluster, one of the files is good because its data is on that shared cluster. However, the second file now has some of the first file's data, corrupting the second file.

The goal is to make a list of all these files and copy them one at a time to a floppy disk. Generally, you can rescue some data by copying to a floppy disk any files that CHKDSK indicates are bad.

The least serious of the error messages is Contains 2 non-contiguous blocks. This message indicates that files are broken into noncontiguous clusters or fragmented on the hard disk. After the disk has been used for a period of time, its files are broken up by DOS to fit into the available free space on the disk. The result can be slower disk performance because the disk heads must move back and forth more on the disk to read the files. In contrast, disks with nonfragmented files read the files in sequence from a small physical area on the disk, minimizing head movement and increasing performance.

If you have Norton Utilities, Mace Utilities, or PC Tools, you may use a disk defragmenter, a program that moves files on your hard disk so that they are contiguous rather than scattered. Using a disk defragmenter increases disk performance by minimizing the time it takes to read an entire file, piece by piece, and minimizes the chance for file errors that may occur when a file is badly fragmented.

After you have identified all the files with problems by using the CHKDSK command, copy the files one at a time to a floppy disk. Then erase them from the hard disk. Examine the copies on the floppy disk to see which are good and which are bad. Before copying the files on the floppy back to the hard disk, perform

CHKDSK *.* /F

Doing so fixes the errors. Fewer errors should be encountered if you have erased all the bad files from the hard disk, but the `29 lost clusters found in 7 chains. Convert lost chains to files (Y/N)? 29696 bytes disk space would be freed` message remains until the lost chains are translated into files.

People often wonder what causes the `lost chains` message. The answer is simple: if you use a program that swaps data between RAM and the drive and you don't exit that program gracefully, you end up creating lost clusters.

What is an ungraceful exit? Powering off the computer or rebooting before exiting the program is a good example. Such a practice creates lost chains. Lost chains are common if you use dBASE IV, WordPerfect 5, or other programs that swap data between the disk and RAM.

Using RECOVER

RECOVER is different from CHKDSK in that it tries to read sectors that have gone bad. When your hard disk takes a long time to read a file and seems to struggle at one particular point, you need to use RECOVER.

Note: RECOVER does not fix problems that should be fixed by CHKDSK. You should run CHKDSK to correct those errors before running RECOVER.

The syntax for RECOVER is

RECOVER *d:path\filename.ext*

where *d:path* is the subdirectory that contains the files to recover and *filename.ext* is the file to recover.

Another form is

RECOVER *d:*

where *d:* is the disk to recover. *Warning:* Use this command only in drastic situations. When RECOVER is run on an entire disk, all files are renamed in a sequential fashion: FILE0000.REC, FILE0001.REC, FILE0002.REC, and so on. All files from subdirectories are brought to the root directory in the same sequential naming system. More files may be on the disk than will fit in the root directory. If this is the case, RECOVER simply stops.

While reading a file from a disk, RECOVER may find a sector that returns a bad Error Correcting Code (ECC) when read by DOS. RECOVER then marks the sector as bad so that it is not reused when other files are stored on the hard disk.

If, for example, while accessing the file LETTER.TXT, you receive the message `Data error reading drive C:` type the command

RECOVER LETTER.TXT

The bad portion of the disk will be marked, and as much of the file as possible will be recovered. Following the RECOVER procedure, check LETTER.TXT to see what was lost.

Recovering a Reformatted Disk

DOS uses the FORMAT command to create the directory and FAT for the disk. When FORMAT is performed, data is not actually removed from the disk. FORMAT replaces the directory and FAT with a new, empty directory and FAT. Therefore, if a disk is accidentally formatted, the data may be recovered. Norton Utilities, Mace Utilities, and PC Tools are all utility programs providing software that makes copies of both the directory and FAT on your hard disk as a specially named file. These utility programs also have other programs that look for those specific files and then use those files to replace the empty directory and FAT.

The data in your directory and FAT is recovered from the copy that was made when you last ran the utility programs that copied the directory and FAT for recovery from an accidental format (usually the last time you rebooted your system, if you ran those programs in your AUTOEXEC.BAT file). Any current changes written to the drive, therefore, may be lost.

Further, if you attempt to place new data on the disk (by trying in any way to write to the disk), you may corrupt the current data on the disk. The reason is that the new data may be stored in the same sectors used by the files containing the backup copies of the directory and FAT.

Mace Utilities has a program called RXBAK.EXE. This program makes a copy of the directory and FAT. If your hard disk gets reformatted, start DOS from a floppy disk. Run Mace Utilities from a floppy disk and choose the option to unformat the hard disk. This utility will locate the file created by RXBAK.EXE and reconstruct the directory and FAT. You must run RXBAK often so that the directory and FAT will be updated.

Recovering a formatted hard disk with old copies of the directory and FAT can be as damaging as not recovering the hard disk at all.

Protecting Your Hard Disk

The best protection for your hard disk is to lock it up. The AT has a key lock on the front panel for this purpose. Some security and password packages provide a reasonable measure of protection for sensitive data on the hard disk. The IBM PS/2 has password protection built in. You may set the password by using the Reference disk supplied with the computer.

One technique for making the entire disk secure is to encrypt both the directory and the FAT. This procedure prevents any data from being read unless the encryption is decoded. Security with PCs is not just preventing someone from stealing your data but also from destroying it. The best protection for sensitive data is to remove it from your hard disk and lock it up. Also available are software packages specifically aimed at securing the data on your hard disk.

Moving Your Hard Disk

When you move your computer, the heads on the hard disk vibrate because of the jostling received during the move. If the heads receive a significant shock—between 40 to 80 times the force of gravity—the heads can hit the disk surface hard enough to damage the disk and cause data loss. Consequently, you should park the heads before moving the disk.

Far greater risk of disk damage is possible when the heads hit the surface of a rotating disk, because the heads then scrape along part of the surface. The amount of shock that can cause damage to a rotating disk is one to two times the force of gravity. This amount is much less than the force required to damage a nonrotating disk.

Parking the heads does not necessarily keep them from contacting the disk surface; parking merely moves the heads to an area of the disk that contains no data. This area is usually the cylinder closest to the center of the drive. New high-speed hard disks have voice coil controlled heads that automatically retract to a locked position when power is removed from the disk.

Beware of SHIPDISK, the diagnostic program that is supposed to prepare your drive for moving. SHIPDISK is provided by IBM on the diagnostic disk that accompanies your system. The problem is that SHIPDISK is designed to work with the special COMMAND.COM that comes with that disk. When used by itself, SHIPDISK does not necessarily leave the heads in the shipping position. Worse yet, the SHIPDISK program for an XT computer should not be used on your AT computer, and vice-versa. If you run the AT SHIPDISK on an XT, you can lose data from your drive.

Guidelines for Parking Your Hard Disk

Often when you purchase a hard disk, a parking program will accompany the hard disk. If not, find a public domain disk head parking program or use the Mace Utilities head parking program instead of using SHIPDISK. Find a parking program that lets you park

the heads while the computer is in use and then permits
you to start using the computer and the disk without
powering off the computer. Use this type of program to
protect against head crashes while the computer is being
used.

Installing New Versions of DOS

When you're upgrading to a new version of DOS, be
aware that procedures vary between Version 3.3 and 4.0.
Each version is examined in this section.

Upgrading to DOS Version 3.3

To upgrade to DOS Version 3.3, boot your computer
with the DOS 3.3 Startup disk in drive A. When you get
the DOS A> prompt, follow these steps:

1. Transfer the hidden DOS files to the hard disk by
   entering

   SYS C:

2. Replace all DOS files in all subdirectories on your
   hard disk (including files that are marked read-only)
   with the new DOS files by entering

   REPLACE A:*.* C:\ /S /R

3. Add any new DOS files to the directory in which
   you store your DOS program files. If you keep all
   DOS files in the directory C:\DOS, for example,
   enter

   REPLACE A:*.* C:\DOS /A

4. Remove the Startup disk from drive A and replace it
   with the Operating disk. Switch to drive C and set a
   path to your DOS directory by entering

   C:
   PATH C:\DOS

5. Follow steps 2 and 3 to replace old files and place
   new files from the Operating disk to the hard disk.

6. Remove the Operating disk from drive A and reboot
   your computer.

Upgrading to DOS Version 4.0

To upgrade to DOS 4.0, simply place the DOS 4.0 Install disk into drive A and boot your computer. Follow the directions on the screen. When prompted, tell the installation program the name of the directory that contains your DOS files. If you store your DOS files in C:\DOS, for example, enter

C:\DOS

Your old DOS files will be replaced with new versions of the files, and any new DOS programs will be added to your \DOS directory. If you currently have the files AUTOEXEC.BAT and CONFIG.SYS on your hard disk, these will be preserved. Two new files called AUTOEXEC.400 and CONFIG.400 will be created. These files reflect any selections to questions during the installation process. Review these files. You may merge new lines in these files with your versions of AUTOEXEC.BAT and CONFIG.SYS.

BACKING UP AND RESTORING FILES

Do not get lured into a false sense of security. Although hard disks are increasingly reliable, they are not everlasting. In addition to the hazards and problems of everyday computer life, human failures abound. Such failures range from overwriting good files with out-of-date files to erasing all files in the wrong directory or forgetting to save regularly as you work. Backing up disks is an extremely inexpensive form of insurance.

Implementing Backup Standards

Implementation of backup standards and procedures for your hard disk requires choosing the backup type (incremental or total), choosing the backup media (tape, Bernoulli, WORM, or floppy), and identifying how often the backup should be performed. You should back up vital information daily or at least every two days if you are changing information such as accounting records. You should back up less vital, but still important, information every couple of days or at least once a week. Set aside time on a particular day of the week to perform a complete backup of your hard disk. In addition to backing up frequently to protect your files, you should back up your complete hard disk at two other times: when you reorganize your hard disk and when you have heavy fragmentation of the hard disk.

Ensuring Backup Integrity

The integrity of most backups is tested only when you use them to reload data after your disk fails. The best approach is to have three copies of all data. There is a chance that one set of backups you make may be bad. For this reason, you should rotate sets of backup disks. Test the backups by using an option in the special backup software. With Bernoulli Boxes, for example, the COMP (Compare) command can compare all files and give an indication of good or bad backup data.

Types of Backups

You should back up disk contents on a regular basis. Two backup strategies can be used: total and incremental.

Duplicating the Entire Disk: Total Backup

One strategy is to copy everything to backup media, whether on disk or tape. You can perform this procedure as often as you deem necessary, depending on your use of the computer. Two problems with this approach follow:

1. The data retained is only from the point of last backup.

2. When data becomes corrupted without your knowledge, and you back up regularly, you risk destroying all good backups with the corrupted data.

Suppose, for example, that on a LAN, a new cache program was tested that seemed to work properly. After the program was installed, several days passed before someone tried to use archived data files on the hard disk. This person discovered that the files had been corrupted, and, consequently, the data in those files was lost. Several backup copies of the data had been made. When the backups were tested, however, all were found to be defective because the corrupted data was placed on the backup by someone who had followed standard backup procedures.

When backing up, you should use more than one set of backup disks or tapes. Rotate these backups so that you have more than one set of backups on which to rely.

Duplicating Some of the Disk: Incremental Backup

The incremental backup strategy for hard disks is to back up the entire hard disk on a certain date. Then, each day, back up all files that have been added to or changed since that date.

For example, do an entire backup on March 1. Then, each day for the rest of the month, back up all files that have been modified since March 1. Using this approach saves you time, while ensuring a copy of all data.

Saving Work in Progress

As you create various files, make a copy of each from the hard disk. For important files, you may want to make several copies.

Suppose, for example, that only one copy of an important file is on the hard disk, and you are storing fresh work in that single copy. If the power fails just as the data is being written to the disk, you will lose the only copy of your work in RAM, as well as the only copy on the hard disk.

To avoid this problem, keep at least two copies of all work in progress on your disk. Store the new data to one file first and then to another. In this manner, if one file becomes corrupted, the remaining file will still be in excellent shape.

As you create new material and modify previous material, always make a floppy backup. Otherwise, regardless of your backup strategy, your day's or week's work on the hard disk can be lost forever.

Backup Hardware Alternatives

You cannot remove hard disk platters. Therefore, you must transfer information to separate media for backup. Most users use floppy disks to back up their hard disks. Other types of backup media are available and are examined in this section.

Magnetic Tape Backups

You make magnetic tape backups by using special software and a magnetic tape recorder. These tapes are specially designed for computer use and store from 60M to more than 100M of data. Some recorders can be attached to the external connector on the floppy disk controller, but others may require a special interface board. Backup time takes about 20 minutes for a 40M drive.

Bernoulli Box Cartridges

Bernoulli Box cartridges are floppy disks that are popular backup media because of their speed (they seem as fast as many hard disks), ease of use (you may employ the XCOPY command rather than the BACKUP command), and reliability. The newer Bernoulli drives fit in the same mounting as an ordinary 5 1/4-inch floppy drive. The Bernoulli cartridges look like enlarged versions of 3 1/2-inch floppy disks. The cartridges store 10M (the original cartridge), 20M, or 40M (the newest dual 20M cartridge system).

WORMs

WORMs are optical disks that permit you to write data once to the drive and then read the data many times. An optical disk is like a Compact Disk (CD) that uses a laser beam to store hundreds of millions of characters on a removable cartridge. WORMs are ideal for backup because every piece of data written always remains on the optical disk. The principal drawbacks in this case are that optical disks are slower than equivalent magnetic media hard disks, optical disks are costly, and no common standards exist among optical drive manufacturers. Disks or ROM disks made to operate in one drive may not operate in other drives. ROM disks, once written to the first time, are strictly read-only. They cannot be written to again.

Using BACKUP

The DOS BACKUP command is designed to copy the data off your hard disk onto floppy disks. A 20M disk can require as many as 60 floppy disks for an entire backup, if you are using 5 1/4-inch double-sided double-density disks. This is the reason that BACKUP has options for copying only part of the hard disk. At system start-up, make an entire copy of the hard disk; then periodically add to that backup copy as new data is created and stored on the hard disk. Whenever data must be restored to the disk, you can then use the RESTORE command. Remember that BACKUP and RESTORE are a matched set.

The syntax for BACKUP is

> **BACKUP** *d1:path\filename.ext d2:* /S /M /A /F
> /**D:***date* /**T:***time*

where *d1:path\filename.ext* is the drive, path, and file name from which you're backing up and *d2:* is the drive to which you're backing up. The use of wildcards in specifying the file is acceptable.

/S specifies to back up all subdirectories of the designated directory.

/M specifies to back up all files that have been modified since the last backup.

/A appends files to be backed up to the current backup disks.

/F formats a disk found not to be formatted during backup.

/D:*date* specifies that all files with the given date or a later date should be backed up.

/T:*time* backs up all files with the given time or a later time.

Here is an example of a common BACKUP command:

BACKUP C:\TEMP*.* A:\ /S /M /A /F

In this case, files in C:\TEMP are being backed up to the disk in drive A. The /S option tells BACKUP to copy all subdirectories under C:\TEMP as well as the files in C:\TEMP. The /M option tells BACKUP to copy to the disk only files containing the archive bit set. The archive bit is set when a file is created or modified; you reset it by using the BACKUP command. The /A option is crucial here because it tells BACKUP not to destroy the existing files on drive A; /A adds files to a backup. The /F option causes BACKUP to format a disk before using it.

Using RESTORE

RESTORE is the reverse of BACKUP. It returns your files from the backup media to your hard disk.

The syntax for RESTORE is

RESTORE *d1*: *d2:path\filename.ext* /S /P /M /N /B:*date* /A:*date* /L:*time* /E:*time*

where *d1:* is the drive to restore from and *d2:path\filename.ext* is the drive, path, and file name to restore to. Wildcards in the file name are acceptable.

/S restores all subdirectories of the directory given.

/P causes a prompt before restoring a file that has been modified since the last backup or is a read-only file.

/M restores all files modified or erased since the last backup.

/N restores files that no longer exist on the destination drive.

/B:*date* restores files from the backup set with dates on or before the date given.

/A:*date* restores files with dates on or after the given date.

/L:*time* restores files with the time at or later than the given time.

/E:*time* restores files with the time at or earlier than the specified time.

The RESTORE command is most often used as follows:

RESTORE A: C:\TEMP*.* /S /P /M

RESTORE uses drive A as the source for restoring the files to the hard disk C in the TEMP subdirectory. All files are restored in the directory \TEMP and its attached subdirectories because the /S option is specified. The /P option causes RESTORE to prompt you for approval in restoring files that have changed since they were last backed up. This procedure ensures that any recent work is not destroyed. Finally, the /M option tells RESTORE to return all files that have been deleted since the backup and also to restore those files that have been modified since the last backup.

If you have no other method to back up and restore your hard disk data periodically, BACKUP and RESTORE are the tools to use. Incremental backups using BACKUP /S /A /M should be performed daily or after you complete a significant amount of work.

Backing Up with XCOPY

XCOPY is practical if you want to copy less than a full floppy disk of files from several directories. You may work intensively in one or two related subdirectories and not other directories. Instead of using BACKUP, you may prefer to use XCOPY to make a fairly quick copy of your files. This technique has one drawback: the files must fit on one floppy disk. When the destination disk is filled, XCOPY stops. You must change disks and restart the XCOPY process using /P to skip the files you have already copied. If you need more than one floppy disk to back up the files, use BACKUP.

When you have a Bernoulli Box, you can use XCOPY to perform your hard disk backup. You can use the following command:

XCOPY C:\TEMP*.* G:\TEMP /S /E

In this example, XCOPY copies all the files from C:\TEMP to drive G:\TEMP. In the copying process, all subdirectories under C:\TEMP are copied, and because the /E option is also set, empty subdirectories under C:\TEMP are created (if needed). To restore the data, reverse the drive designators in the XCOPY command, as shown in the following example:

XCOPY G:\TEMP*.* C:\TEMP /S /E

You can shorten the backup process with XCOPY by using the /M parameter. /M tells XCOPY to copy only those files that have the archive bit turned on. The selection is made from the file's archive bit.

ERROR MESSAGES

The actual wordings of hard disk error messages for your implementation and version of DOS may differ from those listed in this section. Sometimes the differences may be as slight as punctuation and capitalization. Other times, the entire content of the message may differ. If you see a message that you cannot locate in this guide, refer to your computer's DOS manual. For a detailed explanation of CHKDSK error messages, see the earlier section "Analyzing Your Hard Disk."

In the list that follows, hard disk error messages that usually appear when you start MS-DOS are marked (start-up). Most start-up errors indicate that DOS did not start and that you must reboot the system. Most of the other error messages indicate that DOS terminated (aborted) the program and returned to the system prompt (C>). The messages are listed in alphabetical order for easy reference.

Bad call format

A device driver was given a requested header with an incorrect length. The problem is with the applications software making the call.

Bad command

The device driver issued an invalid or unsupported command to the device. The problem may be with the device driver software or with other software trying to use the device driver.

Bad command or filename

ERROR: The name you entered is not valid for invoking a command, program, or batch file. The most frequent causes are the following:

- You misspelled something.

- You omitted a needed drive or path name.

- You gave the parameters without the command name, such as typing **myfile** rather than **ws myfile** (omitting the ws for WordStar).

Check the spelling on the command line. Make sure that the command, program, or batch file is in the location specified (drive and directory path). Then try the command again.

Bad format call

The device driver at fault passed an incorrect header length to DOS. If you wrote this device driver, you must rewrite it to correct the problem. For a purchased program, contact the dealer or publisher who sold you the driver.

Bad or missing Command Interpreter

ERROR (start-up): DOS cannot find the command interpreter, COMMAND.COM. DOS does not start.

This message indicates that COMMAND.COM is not on your hard disk or that the version of COMMAND.COM on the disk is from an earlier DOS version. If you have used the SHELL directive of CONFIG.SYS, the message indicates that the directive is improperly phrased or that COMMAND.COM is not where you specified. Place a disk that contains the operating system into drive A and then reset the system. After DOS has started, copy COMMAND.COM from drive A to your hard disk and reboot.

If resetting the system does not solve your problem, use a copy of your DOS master disk to restart the computer. Copy COMMAND.COM from this disk to the offending disk.

Bad or missing filename

WARNING (start-up): DOS was requested to load a device driver that could not be located. An error occurred when the device driver was loaded, or a break address for the device driver was out of bounds for the size of RAM memory being used in the computer. DOS will continue its boot but will not use the device driver file name.

If DOS loads, check your CONFIG.SYS file for the line DEVICE=filename. Make sure that the line is spelled correctly and that the device driver is where you specified. If this line is correct, reboot the system. If the message appears again, copy the file from its original disk to the hard disk and reboot. If the error persists, contact the dealer or publisher that sold you the driver, because the device driver is defective.

Bad unit

An invalid subunit number was passed to the device driver. The problem may be with the device driver software or with other software trying to use the device driver. Contact the dealer who sold you the device driver.

Batch file missing

ERROR: DOS could not find the batch file it was processing. The batch file may have been erased or renamed. For DOS Version 3.0 only, the disk containing the batch file may have been changed.

DOS aborts the processing of the batch file.

If you are using DOS Version 3.0 and you changed the
disk containing the batch file, restart the batch file and
do not change the disk. You may need to edit the batch
file so that you will not need to change disks.

If you renamed the batch file, rename it again, using the
original name. If required, edit the batch file to ensure
that the file name does not get changed again.

If the file was erased, re-create the batch file from its
backup file if possible. Edit the file to ensure that the
batch file does not erase itself.

Cannot load COMMAND, system halted

ERROR: DOS attempted to reload COMMAND.COM,
but the area where DOS keeps track of available and
used memory was destroyed, or the command processor
was not found in the directory specified by the
COMSPEC= entry. The system halts.

This message indicates either that COMMAND.COM
has been erased from the hard disk's root directory or
that the COMSPEC= entry in the environment has been
changed. Reboot your system. If your system does not
start, the copy of COMMAND.COM has been erased.
Restart from the original master disks and copy
COMMAND.COM to your hard disk.

Cannot start COMMAND, exiting

ERROR: DOS was directed to load an additional copy
of COMMAND.COM but could not. Either your
CONFIG.SYS FILES= command is set too low or
you do not have enough free memory for another copy
of COMMAND.COM.

If your system has 256K or more and the value for
FILES is less than 10, edit the CONFIG.SYS file on
your hard disk and use **FILES=15** or **FILES=20**. Then
reboot.

If the problem occurs again, you do not have enough
memory in your computer or you have too many
resident or background programs competing for memory
space. Reboot again and do not load any resident or
background programs that you do not need. If necessary,
eliminate unneeded device drivers or RAM disk

software. Another alternative is to increase the amount of RAM memory in your system.

Configuration too large

ERROR (start-up): DOS could not load itself because you specified too many FILES or BUFFERS in your CONFIG.SYS file. This problem should occur only on 128K or 192K systems.

Restart with a different disk and edit your CONFIG.SYS file, lowering the number of FILES and/or BUFFERS. Reboot again.

Another alternative is to increase the RAM memory in your system.

Current drive is no longer valid

WARNING: You have set the system prompt to PROMPT $p. At the system level, DOS attempted to read a drive that wasn't ready.

If the current drive is set for a floppy disk, this warning appears when you do not have a disk in the drive. DOS reports a Drive not ready error. Give the A (Abort) command or the I (Ignore) command. Then insert a floppy disk into the drive.

The invalid drive error also can occur if you have a current networked or SUBST drive that has been deleted or disconnected. Simply change the current disk to a valid drive.

Data error reading/writing drive d:

DOS could not read or write the data correctly. Usually the disk has developed a defective spot.

Disk boot failure

ERROR (start-up): An error occurred when DOS tried to load itself into memory. The disk contained IO.SYS and MSDOS.SYS, but one of the two files could not be loaded. DOS did not boot.

Try rebooting again. If the error recurs, try booting DOS from a disk you know is good, such as a copy of your

DOS master disk. If this action fails, you have a
hardware drive problem. Contact your local dealer.

Divide overflow

ERROR: A program attempted to divide by zero.

DOS aborts the program. Either the program was
entered incorrectly, or it has a logic flaw. With well-
written programs, this error should never occur. If you
wrote the program, correct the error and try the program
again. If you purchased the program, report the problem
to the dealer or publisher.

This message also can appear when you are attempting
to format a RAM disk. Make sure that you are
formatting the correct disk and try again.

Drive not ready

An error occurred while DOS tried to read or write to
the drive. For floppy drives, the drive door may be open,
the disk may not be inserted, or the disk may not be
formatted. For hard drives, the drive may not be
prepared properly, or you may have a hardware problem.

Error in EXE file

ERROR: DOS detected an error while attempting to load
a program stored in an EXE file. The problem is in the
relocation information DOS needs to load the program.
This problem can occur if the EXE file has been altered
in any way.

Reboot and try the program again, this time using a
backup copy of the program. If the message reappears,
the program is flawed. If you are using a purchased
program, contact the dealer or publisher. If you wrote
the program, use LINK to produce another copy of the
program.

Error loading operating system

ERROR (start-up): A disk error occurred while DOS
was loading itself from the hard disk. DOS does not
boot.

Restart the computer. If the error occurs after several
tries, restart DOS from the floppy drive. If the hard disk
does not respond (that is, you cannot run DIR or
CHKDSK without getting an error), you have a problem
with your hard disk. Contact your local dealer. If the
hard disk does respond, use the SYS command to put
another copy of DOS onto your hard disk. You also may
need to copy COMMAND.COM to the hard disk.

EXEC failure

ERROR: DOS encountered an error while reading a
command or program from the disk, or the
CONFIG.SYS FILES= command has a value that is
too low.

Increase the number of FILES in the CONFIG.SYS file
of your start-up disk to 15 or 20; then reboot. If the error
recurs, you may have a problem with the disk. Use a
backup copy of the program and try again. If the backup
copy works, copy it over the offending copy.

If an error occurs in the copying process, you have a
flawed floppy or hard disk. If the problem is a floppy
disk, copy the files from the flawed disk to another disk
and reformat or retire the original disk. If the problem is
the hard disk, immediately back up your files and run
RECOVER on the offending file. If the problem persists,
your hard disk may have a hardware failure.

FCB unavailable

With the file-sharing program (SHARE.EXE) loaded, a
program that uses the DOS Version 1.0 method of file-
handling attempted to open concurrently more file
control blocks than were specified with the FCBS
command.

Use the Abort option (see the end of this section).
Increase the value of the FCBS CONFIG.SYS command
(usually by four) and reboot. If the message appears
again, increase the number and reboot.

File allocation table bad, drive d. Abort, Retry, Fail?

WARNING: DOS encountered a problem in the FAT of the disk in drive D. Press **R** for Retry several times. If this action does not solve the problem, use **A** for Abort.

If you are using a floppy disk, attempt to copy all the files to another disk and then reformat or retire the original disk. If you are using a hard disk, back up all files on the disk and reformat the hard disk. The disk is unusable until it is reformatted.

File creation error

ERROR: A program or DOS attempted to add a new file to the directory or replace an existing file, but failed.

If the file already exists, use the **ATTRIB** command to check whether the file is marked as read-only. If the read-only flag is set and you want to change or erase the file, use ATTRIB to remove the read-only flag and then try again.

If the problem is not a read-only flag, run **CHKDSK** without the /F switch to determine whether the directory is full, the disk is full, or some other problem exists with the disk.

File not found

ERROR: DOS could not find the file you specified. The file is not on the correct disk or in the correct directory; or you misspelled the drive name, path name, or file name. Check these possibilities and try the command again.

Filename device driver cannot be initialized

WARNING (start-up): In CONFIG.SYS, either the parameters in the device driver file name are incorrect or the DEVICE line is in error. Check for incorrect parameters and check for phrasing errors in the DEVICE line. Edit the DEVICE line in the CONFIG.SYS file, save the file, and reboot.

General failure

This is a catchall error message not covered elsewhere.
The error usually occurs when you use an unformatted
floppy or hard disk or when you leave the drive door
open.

Incorrect MS-DOS version

ERROR: The copy of the file holding the command you
just entered is from a different version of DOS.

Get a copy of the command from the correct version of
DOS (usually from your copy of the DOS master disk)
and try the command again. If the hard disk or floppy
disk you are using has been updated to hold new
versions of the DOS programs, copy those versions over
the old ones.

Insert disk with \COMMAND.COM in drive d and strike any key when ready

INFORMATIONAL and WARNING: DOS needed to
reload COMMAND.COM but could not find it on the
start-up disk.

If you are using floppy disks, the disk in drive A has
probably been changed. Place a disk holding a good
copy of COMMAND.COM into drive A and press a
key.

Insert disk with batch file and strike any key when ready

INFORMATIONAL: DOS is attempting to execute the
next command from a batch file, but the disk holding the
batch file was removed from the drive. This message
occurs for DOS Version 3.1. DOS Version 3.0 gives a
fatal error when the disk is changed.

Put the disk holding the batch file into the drive and
press a key to continue.

Insert diskette for drive d and strike any key when ready

INFORMATIONAL: You or one of your programs specified a drive that is different from the current drive.

If the correct disk is in the drive, press a key. Otherwise, put the correct disk into the drive and then press a key.

Insufficient disk space

WARNING or ERROR: The disk does not have enough free space to hold the file being written. All DOS programs terminate when this problem occurs, but some non-DOS programs continue.

If you think that the disk has enough room to hold this file, run **CHKDSK** to see whether the hard disk or floppy has a problem. Sometimes when you terminate programs early by pressing Ctrl-Break, DOS is not allowed to do the necessary cleanup work. When this happens, disk space is temporarily trapped. CHKDSK can "free" these areas.

If you simply run out of disk space, free some disk space or use a different disk. Try the command again.

Insufficient memory

ERROR: The computer does not have enough free RAM memory to execute the program or command.

If you loaded a resident program like PRINT, GRAPHICS, SideKick, or ProKey, restart DOS and try the command before loading any resident program. If this method fails, remove any unneeded device driver or RAM-disk software from the CONFIG.SYS file and reboot again. If this action fails, your computer does not have enough memory for this command. You must increase your RAM memory to run the command.

Intermediate file error during pipe

ERROR: DOS is unable to create or write to one or both of the intermediate files it uses when piping (|) information between programs. The disk or root directory is full, or DOS cannot locate the files. The most frequent cause is running out of disk space.

Run the **DIR** command on the root directory of the
current drive. Make sure that you have enough free
space and enough room in the root directory for two
additional files. If you do not have enough room, create
room on the disk by deleting, or copying and deleting,
files. You also may copy the necessary files to a
different disk with sufficient room.

One possibility is that a program is deleting files,
including the temporary files DOS uses. If this is the
case, you should correct the program, contact the dealer
or program publisher, or avoid using the program with
piping.

Internal stack overflow system halted

ERROR: Your programs and DOS have exhausted the
stack, the memory space that is reserved for temporary
use. This problem is usually caused by a rapid
succession of hardware devices demanding attention
(interrupts). If you want to prevent this error from
occurring at all, add the STACKS directive to your
CONFIG.SYS file. If the directive is already in your
CONFIG.SYS file, then increase the number of stacks
specified.

Invalid COMMAND.COM in drive d

WARNING: DOS tried to reload from the disk in
drive D and found that the file was of a different version
of DOS. You will see a message instructing you to insert
a disk with the correct version and press a key. Follow
the directions for that message.

If you frequently use the disk that was originally in the
drive, copy the correct version of COMMAND.COM to
that disk.

Invalid COMMAND.COM, system halted

ERROR: DOS could not find COMMAND.COM on the
hard disk. DOS halts and must be restarted.

COMMAND.COM may have been erased, or the
COMSPEC= setting in the environment may have been
changed. Reboot. If you see a message indicating that

COMMAND.COM is missing, that file was erased.
Restart DOS from a floppy disk and recopy
COMMAND.COM to the root directory of the hard disk
or to wherever your SHELL command directs, if you
have used this command in your CONFIG.SYS file.

If you reboot and this message appears later, a program
or batch file is erasing COMMAND.COM or is altering
the COMSPEC= parameter. If a batch file is erasing
COMMAND.COM, edit the batch file. If a program is
erasing COMMAND.COM, contact the dealer or
publisher that sold you the program. If COMSPEC= is
being altered, either edit the offending batch file or
program, or place COMMAND.COM in the
subdirectory your program or batch file expects.

Invalid directory

ERROR: One of the following errors occurred:

- You specified a directory name that does not exist.

- You misspelled the directory name.

- The directory path is on a different disk.

- You forgot to give the path character (\) at the
  beginning of the name.

- You did not separate the directory names with the
  path character.

Check your directory names, ensure that the directories
do exist, and try the command again.

Invalid drive in search path

WARNING: One specification you gave to the PATH
command has an invalid drive name, or a named drive is
nonexistent or hidden temporarily by a SUBST or JOIN
command.

Use PATH to check the paths you instructed DOS to
search. If you gave a nonexistent drive name, use the
PATH command again and enter the correct search
paths. If the problem is temporary because of a SUBST
or JOIN command, you can again use PATH to enter the
paths but leave out or correct the wrong entry.

Invalid drive specification

ERROR: This message occurs for one of the following reasons:

- You entered the name of an invalid or nonexistent drive as a parameter to a command.

- You have given the same drive for the source and destination, which is not permitted for the command.

- By not giving a parameter, you have defaulted to the same source and destination drive.

Remember that certain DOS commands (such as SUBST and JOIN) temporarily hide drive names while the command is in effect. Check the drive names. If the command is objecting to a missing parameter and defaulting to the wrong drive, explicitly name the correct drive.

Invalid drive specification
Specified drive does not exist,
or is non-removable

ERROR: One of the following errors occurred:

- You gave the name of a nonexistent drive.

- You named the hard disk when using commands for floppies only.

- You did not give a drive name and defaulted to the hard disk when using commands for floppies only.

- You named or defaulted to a RAM drive when using commands for a "real" floppy disk only.

Remember that certain DOS commands (such as SUBST and JOIN) temporarily hide drive names while the command is in effect. Check the drive name you gave and try the command again.

Invalid environment size specified

WARNING: You have given the SHELL directive in CONFIG.SYS. The environment-size switch (/E:*size*) contains either nonnumeric characters or a number that is less than 160 or greater than 32,768.

If you are using the **SHELL** /E:*size* switch of DOS
Version 3.1, *size* is the number of 16-byte memory
blocks, not the number of bytes.

Check the form of your CONFIG.SYS SHELL directive;
the form needs to be exact. A colon should be between
/E and *size*; no comma or space should be between or
within the /E: and the *size* characters; and the number in
size should be greater than or equal to 160, but less than
or equal to 32,768.

Invalid number of parameters

ERROR: You have given either too few or too many
parameters to a command. One of the following errors
occurred:

- You omitted required information.

- You forgot a colon immediately after the drive
  name.

- You put a space in the wrong place or omitted a
  needed space.

- You forgot to place a slash (/) in front of a switch.

Invalid parameter
Incorrect parameter

ERROR: At least one parameter you entered for the
command is not valid. One of the following occurred:

- You omitted required information.

- You forgot a colon immediately after the drive
  name.

- You put a space in the wrong place or omitted a
  needed space.

- You forgot to place a slash (/) in front of a switch.

- You used a switch the command does not recognize.

Invalid partition table

ERROR (start-up): While you were attempting to start
DOS from the hard disk, DOS detected a problem in the
hard disk's partition information.

Restart DOS from a floppy disk. Back up all files from
the hard disk if possible. Run **FDISK** to correct the
problem. If you change the partition information, you
must reformat the hard disk and restore all its files.

Invalid path

ERROR: One of the following errors has occurred to a
path name you have entered:

• The path name contains illegal characters.

• The name has more than 63 characters.

• You specified a directory name that does not exist.

• You misspelled the directory name.

Check the spelling of the path name. If needed, do a
DIR of the disk and ensure that the directory you have
specified does exist and that you have the correct path
name. Be sure that the path name contains 63 characters
or fewer. If necessary, change the current directory to a
directory "closer" to the file and shorten the path name.

Invalid STACK parameter

WARNING (start-up): One of the following errors has
occurred to the STACKS directive in your
CONFIG.SYS file:

• A comma is missing between the number of stacks
and the size of the stack.

• The number of stack frames is not in the range of 8
to 64.

• The stack size is not in the range of 32 to 512.

• You have omitted either the number of stack frames
or the stack size.

• Either the stack frame or the stack size (but not
both) is 0. DOS continues to start but ignores the
STACKS directive.

Check the STACKS directive in your CONFIG.SYS
file. Edit and save the file and then reboot.

Invalid switch character

WARNING: You have used VDISK.SYS in your
CONFIG.SYS file. VDISK encountered a switch (/), but
the character immediately following it was not an *E* for
extended memory. DOS loads VDISK and attempts to
install VDISK in low (nonextended) memory. You
either have misspelled the */E* switch or have left a space
between the / and the *E*. Edit and save your
CONFIG.SYS file and then reboot.

Lock violation

With the file-sharing program (SHARE.EXE) or
network software loaded, one of your programs
attempted to access a file that is locked. Your best
choice is **R**etry. Then try **A**bort. If you choose **A**
however, any data in memory is lost.

Memory allocation error Cannot load COMMAND, system halted

ERROR: A program destroyed the area where DOS
keeps track of in-use and available memory. You must
reboot so that DOS can rebuild this area.

If this error occurs again with the same program, the
program has a flaw. Use a backup copy of the program.
If the problem persists, contact the dealer or program
publisher.

Missing operating system

ERROR (start-up): The DOS hard disk partition entry is
marked as "bootable" (capable of starting DOS), but the
DOS partition does not have a copy of DOS on it.
Therefore, DOS does not boot.

Start DOS from a floppy disk. At the A> prompt, type
SYS C:. Then copy COMMAND.COM from the floppy
to the hard disk.

No free file handles Cannot start COMMAND, exiting

ERROR: DOS could not load an additional copy of
COMMAND.COM because no file handles (indicated

by FILES= in your CONFIG.SYS file) were available.

Edit the CONFIG.SYS file on your start-up disk to increase the number of file handles (using the FILES command) by five. Reboot and try the command again.

Non-DOS disk

The FAT has invalid information. This disk is unusable. You can Abort and run CHKDSK on the disk to see whether any corrective action is possible. If CHKDSK fails, your other alternative is to reformat the disk. Reformatting, however, will destroy any remaining information on the disk. If you use more than one operating system, the disk has probably been formatted under the operating system you are using and should not be reformatted.

Non-System disk or disk error Replace and strike any key when ready

ERROR (start-up): Your floppy or hard disk does not contain DOS, or a read error occurred when you started the system. DOS does not boot.

If you are using a floppy disk system, place a bootable disk into drive A and press a key.

The most frequent cause of this message on hard disk systems is that you left a nonbootable disk in drive A with the door closed. Open the door to drive A and press a key. DOS will boot from the hard disk.

Not enough memory

ERROR: The computer does not have enough free RAM memory to execute the program or command.

If you loaded a resident program like PRINT, GRAPHICS, SideKick, or ProKey, reboot and try the command again before loading any resident program. If this method fails, remove any unneeded device driver or RAM-disk software from the CONFIG.SYS file and restart DOS again. If this option fails also, your computer does not have enough memory for this command. You must increase your RAM memory to run the command.

Not ready

The device (such as your printer or disk drive) is not ready and cannot receive or transmit data. Check the connections, make sure that the power is on, and check whether the device is ready.

Out of environment space

WARNING: DOS is unable to add any more strings from the SET command to the environment. Therefore, the environment cannot be expanded. This error occurs when you load a resident program, such as MODE, PRINT, GRAPHICS, SideKick, or ProKey.

If you are running DOS Version 3.1 or later, refer to the SHELL command for information about expanding the default space for the environment. DOS Version 3.0 has no method to expand the environment.

Path not found

ERROR: A file or directory path you named does not exist. You may have misspelled the file name or directory name, or you omitted a path character (\) between directory names or between the final directory name and file name. Another possibility is that the file or directory does not exist in the area you specified. Check these possibilities and try again.

Path too long

ERROR: You have given a path name that exceeds the 63-character limit of DOS. The name is too long, or you omitted a space between file names. Check the command line. If the phrasing is correct, you must change to a directory that is closer to the file you want and try the command again.

Program too big to fit in memory

ERROR: The computer does not have enough memory to load the program or command you invoked.

If you have any resident programs loaded (such as
PRINT, GRAPHICS, or SideKick), reboot and try the
command again without loading the resident programs.
If this message appears again, reduce the number of
buffers (BUFFERS=) in the CONFIG.SYS file,
eliminate unneeded device drivers or RAM-disk
software, and reboot again. If these actions do not solve
the problem, your computer does not have enough RAM
memory for the program or command. You must
increase the amount of RAM memory in your computer
to run this command.

Read fault

DOS was unable to read the data, usually from a hard
disk or floppy. Check the drive doors and be sure that
the disk is inserted properly.

Sector not found

The drive was unable to locate the sector on the floppy
disk or hard disk platter. This error is usually the result
of a defective spot on the disk or of defective drive
electronics. Some copy-protection schemes use this
method (an intentional defective spot) to prevent
unauthorized duplication of the disk.

Sector size too large in file
filename

WARNING: The device driver is inconsistent. The
device driver defined a particular sector size to DOS but
attempted to use a different size. The copy of the device
driver is bad, or the device driver is incorrect. Copy a
backup of the device driver to the boot disk and then
reboot. If the message appears again, the device driver is
incorrect. If you wrote the driver, correct the error. If
you purchased the program, contact the dealer or
software publisher.

Seek

The drive could not locate the proper track on the floppy
or hard disk platter. This error is usually caused by a
defective spot on the disk or hard disk platter, an
unformatted disk, or drive electronics problems.

Sharing violation

WARNING: With the file-sharing program (SHARE.EXE) or network software loaded, you or one of your programs attempted to access a file by using a sharing mode not allowed at that time. Another program or computer has temporary control over the file.

You will see the message Abort, Retry, Ignore. Choose **R** for Retry several times. If the problem persists, choose **A** for Abort. If you abort, however, any data currently being manipulated by the program is lost.

Syntax error

ERROR: You phrased a command improperly by doing one of the following:

• Omitting needed information

• Giving extraneous information

• Putting an extra space in a file name or path name

• Using an incorrect switch

Check the command line for these possibilities and try the command again.

Too many block devices

WARNING (start-up): Too many DEVICE directives are in your CONFIG.SYS file. DOS continues to start but does not install any additional device drivers.

DOS can handle only 26 block devices. The block devices created by the DEVICE directives plus the number of block devices automatically created by DOS exceeds this number. Remove any unnecessary DEVICE directives in your CONFIG.SYS file and restart DOS.

Top level process aborted, cannot continue

ERROR (start-up): COMMAND.COM or another DOS command detected a disk error, and you chose the **A** (Abort) option. DOS cannot work properly, and the system halts.

Try rebooting. If the error recurs, use a floppy disk to
start DOS. After DOS has started, use the SYS
command to put another copy of the operating system on
the hard disk and copy COMMAND.COM to the disk. If
DOS reports an error during the copying, the disk is bad.
Back up the entire hard disk and then reformat it.

Unable to create directory

ERROR: Either you or a program has attempted to
create a directory, and one of the following has
occurred:

- A directory by the same name already exists.

- A file by the same name already exists.

- You are adding a directory to the root directory, and
  the root directory is full.

- The directory name has illegal characters or is a
  device name.

Do a **DIR** of the disk. Make sure that no file or directory
already exists with the same name. If you are adding the
directory to the root directory, move (COPY and then
erase) or remove any unneeded files or directives. Check
the spelling of the directory and ensure that the
command is phrased properly.

Unrecognized command in CONFIG.SYS

WARNING (start-up): DOS detected an improperly
phrased directive in CONFIG.SYS. The directive is
ignored, and DOS continues to start, but DOS does not
indicate the incorrect line. Examine the CONFIG.SYS
file, looking for improperly phrased or incorrect
directives. Edit the line, save the file, and reboot.

Write fault

DOS could not write the data to this device. Perhaps you
inserted the disk improperly, or you left the drive door
open. Another possibility is an electronics failure in the
floppy or hard drive. The most frequent cause is a bad
spot on the disk.

Write protect

The floppy disk is write-protected.

Note: One of the previously listed error messages (usually `Data`, `Read fault`, or `Write fault`) appears when you are using a double-sided disk in a single-sided drive or a 9-sector disk (Version 2.0 and later) with a version of DOS Version 1.0. DOS will display one of these error messages followed by the line

```
Abort, Retry, Ignore?
```

If you press **A** for Abort, DOS ends the program that requested the read or write condition. Pressing **R** for Retry causes DOS to try the operation again. If you press **I** for Ignore, DOS skips the operation and the program continues. However, some data may be lost when Ignore is used.

The order of preference, unless stated differently under the message, is **R**, **A**, and **I**. You should retry the operation at least twice. If the condition persists, you must decide whether to abort the program or ignore the error. If you ignore the error, data may be lost. If you abort, data still being processed by the program and not yet written to the disk will be lost. Remember that **I** is the least desirable option and that **A** should be used after **R** has failed at least twice.

PUBLIC DOMAIN SOFTWARE

Many public domain programs can help with hard disk management. Some of the programs have been around for a long time and have worked with multiple versions of DOS; these programs are examined in this section. Some of the oldest programs perform key tasks very reliably and predictably.

You can obtain a public domain program free of charge from a computer bulletin board or local users' group. You also may obtain these programs for a minor charge ($2 to $3) from a public domain software house.

ATTR.COM

ATTR changes file attributes, including the system and read-only attributes.

BAC.COM

BAC is a program like XCOPY. BAC copies only the changed files from the source to the target drive.

CORETEST.EXE

CORETEST is from CORE International, a seller of high-capacity and high-performance drives. This program measures the performance of your disk and shows how poorly it performs compared with the CORE disks.

DOSEDIT.COM

DOSEDIT is a DOS command line editor. This program is bulletproof. It allows you to edit the DOS command line and pull up previous DOS commands.

FASTKB.COM

FASTKB speeds up the key rate for AT class computers.

KILLDIR.COM

KILLDIR removes directories and makes the job an easy task.

PAK.EXE

PAK is an archiving program that compresses files to a greater extent than comparable archiving programs. PAK is an essential space saver for any hard disk and can give your disk six months more capacity.

PARK.COM

Most hard disk sellers provide this program to park hard disks. PARK is the simplest of all the park programs.

QD.COM

QD (Quick Disk) is a directory program, attribute

changer, file viewer, and so on. It has one small quirk, however. When renaming files, you cannot enter the number 8 directly from the keyboard.

QUICKEYS.COM

QUICKEYS speeds up the key rate for XT class computers.

SEARCH.COM

SEARCH is the best alternative to DOS 3.3 APPEND. It works with earlier versions of DOS and uses less memory than APPEND.

SWEEP.COM

SWEEP is a handy program that causes DOS commands to be executed in every subdirectory on the hard disk. For example, you may use SWEEP to remove all files of a particular type from your hard disk.

TIMEMARK.COM and TIMEPARK.COM

TIMEMARK and TIMEPARK automatically park the heads on your hard disk after a specified time interval. The minimum interval is one minute.

VTREE.COM

VTREE produces a compressed picture of the directory structure of your hard disk.

WHEREIS.COM

WHEREIS is an excellent file-finding program. WHEREIS finds and displays file names in any subdirectory on any disk.

WRITEC.COM

WRITEC is a virus-protection program. When invoked, WRITEC prevents data from being written to the hard disk by making the computer think that the hard disk is a floppy with the write protection tab installed.

PRODUCT RESOURCES

Following is a list of many of the products mentioned in or used during the research of this book. Although every effort has been made to provide a correct listing, Que Corporation cannot attest to the accuracy of this information.

CompuServe Information Services

CompuServe Incorporated
5000 Arlington Centre Blvd., P.O. Box 20212
Columbus, OH 43220
(800) 848-8990 or (614) 457-8650

Time-sharing services and shareware programs.

CoreFast

Microbridge Computers International, Inc.
655 Skyway, Suite 125
San Carlos, CA 94070
(415) 593-8777

Disk backup software.

Disk Optimizer

SoftLogic Solutions
One Perimeter Rd.
Manchester, NH 03103
(603) 627-9900

Disk defragmenter.

FASTBACK/FASTBACK PLUS

Fifth Generation Systems, Inc.
11200 Industriplex Blvd.
Baton Rouge, LA 70809
(504) 291-7221

Disk backup software.

FLASH

Software Masters, Inc.
6352 Guilford Ave.

Indianapolis, IN 46220
(317) 253-8088

Disk cacher, RAM disk, and print spooler.

HTEST/HFORMAT (including HOPTIMUM)

Paul Mace Software, Inc.
400 Williamson Way
Ashland, OR 97520
(503) 488-0224

Low-level disk test-format package.

Mace Utilities/Mace Gold

Paul Mace Software, Inc.
400 Williamson Way
Ashland, OR 97520
(503) 488-0224

Disk utilities package.

Norton Utilities/Norton Commander/Advanced Utilities

Peter Norton Computing, Inc.
2210 Wilshire Blvd., Suite 186
Santa Monica, CA 90403
(213) 319-2000

Disk utilities package.

PC Tools

Central Point Software, Inc.
15220 N.W. Greenbrier Pkwy., #200
Beaverton, OR 97006
(503) 690-8090

Disk utilities package.

SpinRite

Gibson Research Corporation
22991 La Cadena
Laguna Hills, CA 92653
(714) 830-2200

Disk tester and interleave setter.

SAMPLE HIERARCHICAL STRUCTURES

The recommended tree structure for your hard disk is to have as few tree levels as possible. This structure works easily with a wider variety of DOS commands—in particular, those commands designed to work with the floppy drives. Alternative file structures, however, are used for hard disk organization.

One strategy is to separate the programs from the data, using one subdirectory to contain all the data, with individual subdirectories divided by function. This type of structure is ideal for easy backups (see fig. 9).

Another strategy is to separate the programs from the data and to have the data reside in subdirectories assigned to the people using the hard disk. This structure is ideal for a system shared by several users. In this case, paths are used so that different users can run key programs from their individual subdirectories (see fig. 10).

You also can group subdirectories by function. In figure 11, all the information for the marketing department, for example, is stored under one subdirectory, \MKTG. This subdirectory may contain data from various programs.

People using a hard disk can divide their files into data subdirectories for each type of software. Paths are used so that different users can run the programs from data subdirectories assigned to each separate program.

You also can assign the programs to the people using them by placing the programs in subdirectories for the people. Those using the hard disk can have their own program files in program subdirectories for each type of software. In this case, paths are used so that different users can run DOS and other common programs from their subdirectories.

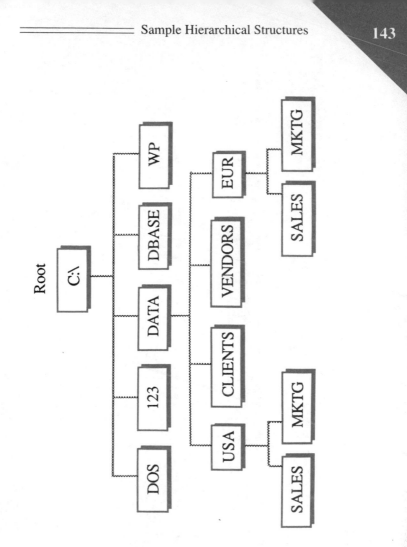

Fig. 9. A sample hierarchical directory structure—ideal for easy backups.

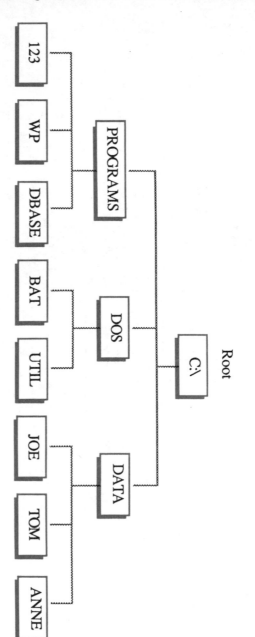

*Fig. 10. A sample hierarchical directory structure—
ideal for a system shared by several users.*

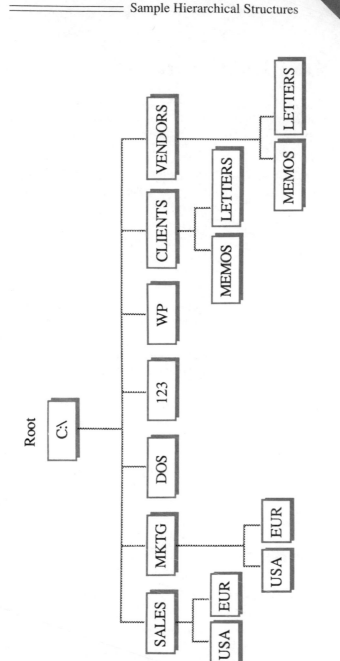

Fig. 11. A sample hierarchical directory structure, grouped by function.

DOS EDITING KEYS

Several function keys can be used at the DOS command line and within some DOS programs such as EDLIN and DEBUG. The DOS editing keys are as follows:

Key	*Use*
F1 or →	Copies the next character from the template to the current command line
F2	Copies all characters from the previous command line—up to but not including the character typed from the template—to the current command line
F3	Copies all remaining characters from the template to the current command line
F4	Deletes all characters from the template up to but not including the next key you type (opposite of F2)
F5	Places the current command line into the template and starts the current command line over
F6	Produces an End-Of-File marker (^Z) when you copy from the console to a disk file
Ins	Enables you to insert characters on the command line without overwriting the template
Del	Deletes a character from the template
Backspace or ←	Deletes the preceding character from the comand line
Esc	Cancels the current command line

Index

Operating Systems

Operating Systems

Upgrading and Repairing PCs

An exceptional reference! *Upgrading and Repairing PCs* helps you troubleshoot common problems and make informed decisions on upgrading any IBM or compatible hardware.

Order #882   **$24.95**

Managing Your Hard Disk, 2nd Edition

Organize the data on your hard disk efficiently and quickly with this valuable text. Also covers DOS 3.3, IBM's PS/2 hardware, and new application and utility software.

Order #837   **$22.95**

Understanding UNIX: A Conceptual Guide, 2nd Edition

Gain an overall perspective on the popular UNIX operating system. Includes a program history, information on the UNIX structure and file system, and a comparison with competitive products.

Order #831   **$21.95**

Using Microsoft Windows

Hands-on practice sessions in this valuable text make it easy for you to manage the Windows interface, control the MS-DOS Executive, and use Windows desktop applications.

Order #804   **$19.95**

Networking IBM PCs, 2nd Edition

Evaluate the major networking systems, then select, install, use, and manage the one that's best for you. *Networking IBM PCs* covers all critical LAN management issues.

Que Order Line: **1-800-428-5331**   Order #71   **$19.95**

Quick Reference Series

The Que *Quick Reference* Series is a portable resource of essential personal computer knowledge compiled in unique, individual guides for your favorite software programs.

1-2-3 Quick Reference

Order #862   **$7.95**

Assembly Language Quick Reference

Order #934   **$7.95**

AutoCAD Quick Reference

Order #979   **$7.95**

C Quick Reference

Order #868   **$7.95**

DOS and BIOS Functions Quick Reference

Order #932   **$7.95**

dBASE IV Quick Reference

Order #867   **$7.95**

Hard Disk Quick Reference

Order #974   **$7.95**

Microsoft Word 5 Quick Reference

Order #976   **$7.95**

MS-DOS Quick Reference

Order #865   **$7.95**

QuickBASIC Quick Reference

Order #869   **$7.95**

Turbo Pascal Quick Reference

Order #935   **$7.95**

WordPerfect Quick Reference

Order #866   **$7.95**